Lisa,

Very nice to "meet" you in this beautiful time and place. In advance, I appreciate your talents of PR and Communication. Look forward to working you

Enjoy

"MEETINGS" AT 35,000 FEET
AND WHAT ARE THEIR "MEANINGS"?

One day we will look back and see the "Meaning" of why we are "Meeting". The Power of the Universe

"MEETINGS" AT 35,000 FEET
AND WHAT ARE THEIR "MEANINGS"?

MY MEMORIES OF TRAVELERS
OVER 28 YEARS

Les Dotson

Dotson Book Publishing, LLC
Miami Beach, Florida

"MEETINGS" AT 35,000 FEET

AND WHAT ARE THEIR "MEANINGS"?

Published by:

Dotson Book Publishing, LLC

trustinfaith@gmail.com

Les Dotson, Publisher

Yvonne Rose, Editor

Quality Press Info, Book Packager

Copyright © 2020 by Les Dotson

Paperback ISBN #: 978-1-7359054-0-2

Ebook ISBN #: 978-1-7359054-1-9

Library of Congress Control Number: 2020919355

DEDICATION

I dedicate this book to God, Jesus Christ's sacrifice, and the Universal connection humanity has and will embrace.

Keep us safe as we travel.

"Meetings" at 35,000 Feet and what are their "meanings"?

ACKNOWLEDGEMENTS

Special Thanks To:

My father and mother, Earl and Nancy Dotson, for having born me into this world and giving me the guidance and structure of life that have set my foundation for the man I am today;

My twin sister, Lisa Chandra Dotson, since we were born of experiencing this life journey of sharing and caring on the same clock, just 4 minutes apart;

My brother, LaMar Cedric Dotson, for the opportunity for us to share and care enough to hear each other out through the trials and tribulations of life, and the importance of being great people, fathers, and grandfathers;

My Dotson/Davis/Ross family members;

My daughter, Alicia, her husband, Ryan Crespin, and his family, for all the years of beautiful friendship;

My daughter's love and blessing of my granddaughter, Kayla Crespin;

Veronica Lopez; I love you;

"Meetings" at 35,000 Feet and what are their "meanings"?

My boys: Rob Williams, Clinton Green, Keith Braesch, Chris Dijkhof, Mukunda Singh, John Williams, Lee Natividad, Stephen Gradney, for being warriors of life and/or prayer partners, Sacred Sons, and part of the men's groups;

Therez Fleetwood and Yvonne Rose, for being such beautiful ladies; wise, strong, and just great writers;

Gina Lopez, for being such a wonderful friend and from "the Raz" where it all began in Carson, California. Thank you so much for the prayer support and dedication; and

Feili Lee, for being such a beautiful soul. I thank you for your support and the support from your family.

CONTENTS

PREFACE

"Meetings" at 35,000 feet, and What are their "Meanings"? is a compilation of my memories of travelers over 28+ years in airplanes, and the beautiful, funny, spiritual, crazy, and eventful stories of people literally "Meeting" at 35,000 feet.

What are the "Meanings" of those "Meetings"? Everyone has their own perspective of what they mean, how they got there at that particular time and place, and why they met that other person or persons. It is a fascinating topic, and many people have great stories to tell about their "Meetings" at 35,000 feet and What the "Meanings" are for them, as well.

The motivation for writing this book came when I sat next to "JW" on a flight from Bradley, CT to Chicago, IL and Chicago, IL to Los Angeles, CA. Little did I know a spiritual awakening would be the result! When I sat next to this gentleman, JW, and looked over at him, I could see he either was tired from a long week of work or was worried about something.

I was tired as well.

When I looked over at his wrist, I noticed that he was wearing a black rubber bracelet, one of those bracelets you get at a charity event or trade show. It had "God is Big Enough" written on it.

JW and Me

We started to speak when I asked him about the bracelet, and the "Meeting" for JW and I began!

In JW's words, and as I also believe, God was the orchestrator of this "Meeting" at 35,000 feet. After this meeting in our personal and business lives, the brother-ship and prayer partner was the "Meaning".

Today, several years later, JW and I keep in touch weekly and encourage each other through spiritual inspirations and messages. *God is good all the time!*

INTRODUCTION

I believe in the universal connections of life; I believe in God. I believe in Jesus. I believe that we are all connected in one way or another, and I believe in equality for the salvation of humanity.

When one of the events in my book happened, I decided that I would act accordingly. With the passage of so many years since then and great spiritual reflection, I feel that now is the right time to re-examine that incident and understand what life is truly about.

I want readers to know that it is fantastic to be fully awake. I don't want to go back to sleep and fool myself into believing things here on Earth are under our complete control because they are not. They are all controlled by high vibrations and low vibrations. High vibrations are forces of positive and good flow, while low vibrations are forces of negative and not-so-good flow). These forces are all intertwined. Life is all about how we interact with those vibrations, whether through people, places, or just environmental things. Whatever the outcome, we must be aware that it is not of our choosing, but rather by living through the experiences created every day. Both vibrations will affect us one way or another in our lives.

The loss this year of Kobe Bryant (41), his daughter Gianna (13), and the seven other beautiful souls - may they rest in peace- is a clear example of beautiful souls that leave this realm in time and transition to a new life pattern after touching so many lives with their good vibrations. Life is too short, and we must live it to the fullest, just like Kobe did. He showed the world what is truly important: family, knowing your purpose, and doing everything you can to positively touch people's lives. I cannot stress this point enough.

CHAPTER 1

THE ULTIMATE "MEETING"
– DIVINE INTERVENTION

On October 3, 1965, I (Leslie Chan Dotson) was born at Daniel Freeman Hospital, in Inglewood, California, along with my twin sister (Lisa Chandra Dotson). We also have a younger brother, LaMar Cedric Dotson, who was born 12 years later. My Dad and Mom were very loving and conscientious parents. I grew up in a middle-class home, where I was raised with a good education, as well as with love, peace, and honor. My childhood days were very happy.

Although our parents, Earl and Nancy Dotson, were both born in the same community in Houston, Texas, they did not know each other before the day they met by divine intervention in 1964, in Los Angeles, California. One day, Nancy was at her church and Earl happened to be visiting. They met in the aisle while on their way to the church altar for prayer. After the church service, they introduced themselves to each other. Earl mentioned that he was the brother of Walter Dotson. Nancy remarked to Earl that he looked just like his brother, Walter. Earl responded, "everyone tells me that most of the time, but I am the older brother."

Nancy and Walter knew each other from Phillis Wheatley Senior High School, Class of 1958, in Houston, Texas. Nancy had never known Earl because after he graduated from Phillis Wheatley Senior High School, Class of 1956, in Houston, Texas, he joined the U.S. Army.

So, Earl and Nancy never connected until years later on that fateful day of their meeting at Nancy's church. Less than two months after their chance meeting, they were married. My twin sister, Lisa Chandra Dotson, and I were born a year and a day later; my parents' wedding anniversary is October 2nd, and our birthday is October 3rd.

October was a fun month in our household!

My Dad is unbelievable in social media and entertainment, and he is highly connected from a social reality standpoint. In the neighborhood, he can walk anywhere, and everyone will know him. For thirty years, my Dad has owned his business - The Way We Were Productions.

My Mom is a very, very strong woman; she is an Aquarian and an unbelievable woman. She knows instinctively how to encourage others to learn, share, care, and use their unique gifts, talents, and skills to help others at home, school, and community. My Mom served the Los Angeles Unified School District for thirty-seven and a half years; she served as a Mathematics/Science Teacher and Mathematics

Teacher/Coordinator at a secondary school site; Secondary Mathematics Adviser at the Area C District Level; and Categorical Programs Adviser/Coordinator at a secondary school site. My Mom is now retired.

My Dad and Mom have been my role models. It is good to have this type of leadership from people who have been very close to you; fortunately, I do not have to go too far to have this type of leadership.

Family Affair: Earl and Nancy Dotson,
Lisa and Lamar Dotson with Les

I grew up in Carson, California, and had a wonderful childhood. The community was very mixed – Whites, Blacks, Hispanics, Filipinos, Samoans, Asians, etc. It was truly remarkable to have that melting pot of people surrounding me daily – so many different cultures and ethnic groups - while growing up. Because of this exposure, I feel that my ability to communicate with diverse people during my travels has been a part of my destiny.

When I was young, I was gifted with musical talent, and I played trumpet. Music excited me - it was my first true love and became a passion for bringing people joy through my music. I was a music major in school and excelled very well, so I performed at lots of events and received many awards. I believe that my experience from being around so many people of different ethnicities, cultures, backgrounds, and lifestyles was cultivated through music because music has no agenda.

When you are playing in an orchestra or band, it doesn't matter if you're White, Brown, or Black. It doesn't matter if you have money or don't, or if you're from the inner- city or a middle-class community. We're all playing the same music, and we're all from the same accord.

Music has good vibrations. As I got older, my musical engagements took me further from my home community and broadened my life scope. My music passion expanded while piquing my curiosity to learn more about the people I played with and performed for. When I was in high school, my friend Jeffrey and I were selected for a special orchestra; two people were chosen from each of the various counties in California. My friend Jeffrey and I were picked for Los Angeles County. Although the orchestra was defined as "multi-cultural", we were the only two African Americans out of about 150 participants. When I look back, I realize that this experience should have been a wake-up call for how these other cultures live and how they differ from one another. But, we all become the same by playing the same music for a few moments in time. So, besides the impact on my childhood, music really impacted my worldview. *I didn't know it at the time, but it was preparing me for my future career.*

Music inspiration as a young man, Georgia on my Mind trumpet solo, 1982 LA Sports Arena,

Carson Colts Baby! Being in the USC
Marching band was terrific, Trojans!

I didn't have any significant conflicts until I was 17 or 18 years old when I met my daughter's mother. Here we see another chance meeting out of the divine, which woke me up, caused reality to kick in, and changed the course of my life. From the moment my daughter's mother became pregnant, there was a massive controversy between my mother and me. My mother had been warning me before anything happened that she wasn't feeling right about this situation. But, I decided to be a knucklehead, and the consequences came. And my new universal direction was set.

I met my daughter's mom through my good friend, Sonny. While I was in my senior year of high school, I worked part-time at Pizza Hut, the after-football game party place back in the day. One day Sonny came to work, crying. I asked him what was wrong, and he told me that his brother had died. I said, "Oh my God!" And he replied, "Yes, my brother drowned, and he had a fiancé and a baby." A few months passed, and one day Sonny wanted to introduce me to his family members. So, he said, "Les, come over to where my brother's ex lives because I think you guys would get along, and she's depressed. Maybe you guys can go out." So, we met, and we clicked and began to hang out. She already had Veronica Lopez (my stepdaughter in spirit), who was Sonny's brother's daughter. Then 8 months later, she became pregnant by me.

Suddenly, my world shifted. I had to decide to be a father and take responsibility… and everything changed for me. So here I was, 19 years old with an un-planned baby despite using birth control. This was God's destiny for us and my life was going in a totally different direction. I would not be graduating from the college of my dreams, USC, and I had to give up the pursuit of a music career to work full-time because I needed to support my child.

Because of my upbringing, I knew that I needed to do the right thing for my daughter and her mother; so, I stepped right in and took responsibility. Alicia's mother and I married, and I was adamant that my baby would be a part of my life and that she would have my name; I set out to do just that. I named my daughter Alicia Leslie Dotson; she was born on May 1, 1986, seven months after my 19th birthday.

While in high school, my clear vision for the future was music. I was entirely into music, loved it, and had a great teacher, Jim Berk. I was part of the Los Angeles Junior Philharmonic, and my trumpet teacher was Greg Hara. *I was truly living my dream, what I thought was my destiny.*

I was very talented and participated in all types of plays and as many things as possible to involve my musical skills. I received a scholarship from Herb Alpert, my mentor in trumpet playing. Thus, it was very traumatic for me to give up my dream of having a career in music.

Sometimes, it's very frustrating to know that you can play an instrument and have this talent but physically can no longer do it. Every once in a while, I try to play my trumpet, but it really hurts my mouth because my teeth have changed. However, on the bright side, I can still play classical piano by ear, which does give me a certain solace.

Fortunately, I had many good people who surrounded me; they loved me and cared about me. My mom and dad were solid and loving; my sister was supportive and always there to help me take care of Alicia whenever I needed her. Veronica's grandmother Carmen was an angel to assist them. I also had a very good support system amongst my friends, so I could get through any trauma that I was experiencing as a teenage father. I also felt that Alicia was like my angel; my family and friends surrounding my baby and me were very protective. Because of my love for Alicia, when many people I knew were doing other things and either getting shot, ending up in jail, or joining the military, I, instead, focused on being a role model for my daughter.

Now that I look back at my youth, I believe that Alicia was like my angel; I realize now that she was given to me to keep me on a path. I was asleep then, but now that I am fully awake, I know that the *real* blessing for me was actually having Alicia. Veronica was the cherry on top as my stepdaughter; now I have my granddaughter, Kayla, and my circle is complete.

"Meetings" at 35,000 Feet and what are their "meanings"?

aliciaeslie25
Kapalua, Hawaii

Alicia Mom, April Sampang, Alicia and Veronica

....and of course, Kayla Crespin, my granddaughter

CHAPTER 2

SMOKEY NEW MEXICO

Scan QR code with phone
To See Chapter Preview

My family has always been close to the church, and as Christians, we love Jesus Christ, who has been a very strong part of my life. That's what my parents instilled in me as a child, and it is still with me today. My belief in God has made me a better person. Without Him, there would be no direction for me; I would just be lost. So, I believe that the angels are here to guide me in the right direction, and I am always protected by God, no matter what. On one particular flight, there was no doubt in my mind that my life was in God's hands and that my fate was His decision.

About 15 years ago, I flew back from New Jersey to LAX to see my family and loved ones. It was a nice flight, flowing smoothly. I was sitting in first class and enjoying a light meal and conversation with the gentleman sitting next to me.

We were halfway through the flight, and all of a sudden, we started to smell a slight "burning" smell. It was very faint but strong enough to tell that something was burning. However, there was no smoke in the cabin.

The Fight Attendants looked puzzled, as well. Then the pilot came on the intercom and said, "I am sorry for the slight burning smell, but we think one of the oxygen sensor fuses blew, and this is causing the smell. There is no need for alarm; everything is okay." The smell should go away in a few minutes. The pilot was right; the smell went away.

Everyone looked at each other, kind of relieved; they shrugged their shoulders and went back to what they were doing. About 30 minutes later, the burning smell became stronger, but there was still no smoke in the air. The people in my area started to panic; one guy told a person to look outside the window to see if the wings were on fire! The guy looked out the window, and he said, "No, the wings look fine." Then someone asked, "What about the other side?" So, the guy sitting next to me lifted up the shade and said, "I don't see anything on this side either...the wings are fine."

You could clearly see by the look on the flight attendants' faces that they had no idea what the hell was going on, and people started to panic...

Suddenly, the plane started to rumble, like a slight shake, then the plane began to dive down! People were screaming and freaking the f**k out. My heart was pounding like crazy, and the first thing I could think of when the air mask dropped was to call my mom. *Now I am dating myself* - they had those phones in the back of the seats, and I immediately picked it up and dialed her as fast as possible. My mom picked up, and I told her in a panicked voice, "I love you. I am on a flight to LA and the plane is going down, and please take care of my daughter Alicia." My mom started screaming, saying, "What is going on?" And I repeated, "Mom, I am on the plane, and it is going down. I love you guys. Tell Alicia I love her and please take care of her." My mom's voice was super nervous, and she said she loved me, and I said, "I have to go! Love you!" The flight attendants went into their usual routine of telling people to sit down, fasten their seatbelts and put away their tray tables, etc. The dive seemed like a long journey, and people were just screaming.

Suddenly, the plane just leveled off out of the dive, but it was still shaking and rumbling. Then the pilot came back on the intercom and said, "I am so sorry, but we had to bring the plane down quickly to a 10,000-feet safety level because the oxygen mechanism totally blew, and we were afraid you wouldn't have been able to breathe at the higher altitude. We will have to do an emergency landing in Albuquerque, New Mexico (hence this story Smokey New Mexico). "Flight attendants, please prepare the cabin and passengers for an emergency landing."

Now, you know, people just went bananas; we all started getting into the crash plane mode. I was freaking out. My heart felt like it was going to burst out of my chest the closer and closer we got to the ground. I looked out the window quickly and could see the fire and rescue trucks' red lights flashing on the runway. The plane was still in a rumble state, as we got closer and closer to the ground. Finally, the plane landed. "BOOM!" It hit the wheels super hard on the ground; probably the hardest I have ever felt a plane land since flying. The pilot got control of the plane as it was swirling back and forth on the runway. Finally, it came to a stop; they popped the emergency doors, and the emergency crews arrived on board to check people.

And this is where the "Meetings" of 245 souls started. The pilot came back onto the intercom again and stated, "I'm sorry for the rough landing. We are safe, and the rescue teams will assist us off the plane." People were cheering and crying with joy to be on the ground and alive. We were still in fright and terror mode, but at the same time, relieved. I have never seen so many men and women crying from pure joy in my life. It was a literal and unified "meeting" of many souls agreeing that life is worth it and cherishing it fully. *This is the "Meaning" of these "Meetings" at 35,000 feet that outlines this book's mantra.*

When we finally got off that plane, they placed us in a holding area for 2.5 hours. It was unbelievable, just listening to the "meetings" that started to happen. There were many stories of joy and relief, and people were repeating over and over: "We could have crashed! We could have died; see, we are all blessed! God spared our lives! God watched over us and saved the plane! We are all blessed!!!" It is incredible to see that when death and tragedy are on us, everyone turns to prayer and to God.

Countless pledges were made by the passengers that day:

- I am going to change my life.
- I am going to spend more time with my family.
- I am not going to work so hard.

- I am not going to take life for granted anymore.

- I am going to live life to the fullest.

- I am going to go and see the places I always wanted to see.

- I will no longer put things off because life is too short, and you just never know.

No one was saying, "oh, let me check my mortgage payment or my car payment or check on my job to see if I have meeting follow-ups." Everyone's reality of true-life stuff was right in front of them – God's love, family, or loved ones and SELF-LOVE.

As soon as we touched down and got settled, I spoke to my family by phone. And all were super relieved that the plane landed okay and that everything was fine. But immediately, it was a thankfulness of God and the Universe that life is not promised to us and that we should cherish life in every way.

That day changed me; it shook me up to my life's reality, and I could see that others were affected the same way. My "Meeting" at 35,000 feet and "Meaning" was that I must always be grateful to God and the Universe. I must live life as if it were my last day, say my prayers, and be thankful for this life that I have been given, now... not later. This was the "Meaning" of my "Meeting" that day, and I will never forget this inflection point that sparked a new appreciation for life. It inspired me to design and to think clearly, and be awake to what is real in life. It taught me to move and communicate differently and to cherish family and loved ones. It taught me to give back and not to be selfish with my time. *It indeed was an awakening from God... and thank you, Jesus Christ. Now when people read this book, they can understand why I am the way I am.*

That flight is one of the reasons that I was reminded to write this book. Thank you, "Smokey New Mexico" for ***"Meetings" at 35,000 feet.*** I will never forget your ***"Meaning."***

CHAPTER 3

MY ANGELS PROTECT
AND GUIDE ME

With so much unrest in the world now due to CV-19, planning a trip by air causes apprehension for many people, sometimes even for me. But ever since "Smokey New Mexico," I am more attuned to the angels of the universe. In particular, Michael and Gabriel continue to pop up in my mind; they are the strongest angels. Based on their roles, I don't feel that their presence is just a coincidence.

In Greek, the word for angel is *aggelos* (pronounced ang-el-os). Its meanings include "a messenger, envoy, one who is sent, a messenger from God".

Michael is called "one of the chief princes," "your prince," and "great prince" (Daniel 10:13, 21; 12:1). His role includes standing as a watchman or guardian over God's people. Michael is the only angel clearly called an archangel

(Jude 9). The word *archangel* in Greek is *archaggelos.* It means "archangel," or "chief of the angels".

Archangel Michael, whose name means 'he who is as God', is most often thought of as the angel of protection and the most powerful of all the angels. He is considered a leader within the angelic realm and a patron angel of righteousness, mercy, and justice. As such, scriptural artwork depicts him as a warrior, most often carrying a sword. Archangel Michael assists situations where you are afraid, confused, or concerned for your safety. He helps to release fear and doubt, supports us in making life changes, and is often said to work closely with those who perform healing work or provide spiritual teaching.

The third highest-ranking angel is Gabriel. Archangel Gabriel's name means 'God is my strength'. One of the two archangels specifically named in the Bible in both the Old and New Testament, Gabriel is often portrayed holding a trumpet and as the only female archangel. As the patron of communications, Archangel Gabriel is the messenger angel, acting as a messenger of God. She helps writers, teachers, journalists, and artists convey their message, find motivation and confidence, and market their skills. She also assists in overcoming issues of fear and procrastination in communication.

Fortunately, I have never been seriously ill; I have had no physical injuries, no hospitalizations, no surgery, no broken bones. With that kind of track record, it's easy to assume that I have a guardian angel. That's very possible, but what I do know is that I have a strong belief in the power and love of

God. Whatever I go through and whatever I am facing, I know God will pull me through if I just ask Him and praise Him.

I think I was about 13 or 14 years old the first time I flew. Our family had to fly to a funeral, so it was a bit traumatic for me and less pleasurable than it might have been if we were traveling for a vacation. I never thought much about flying after that until I started working at Epson in 1987-1988. That was when I really looked forward to the experience of flying internationally and when I became conscious of the benefits of flying.

Throughout my youth, I had lived in a melting pot of many cultures. I realized that my career was giving me the chance to finally discover the roots of many that I had encountered as a youth. I happily seized the opportunity to embark on these international travels. That was when I really embraced flying and the joys associated with it. However, I must clarify that it is the destination that makes me excited, not necessarily the flight!

My first international flight was to Japan. I could finally witness other cultures in person and observe how they lived, worked, and socialized. The Japanese are fascinating, and I have since gained much insight into the many ways their culture differs from ours.

Now, I frequently travel to China and find that the Chinese people are incredible. They are on fire.

All the international flights that I take are thoroughly mixed culturally; this shows the current business world's nature.

I used to take about four domestic flights a month, 48 a year, nearly one a week, but I fly internationally every 8 to 10 weeks. I found myself practically living out of a suitcase, and I stayed tired from jetlag. So, to sum it up, I crisscross across the United States almost weekly, and at least six times a year, I am flying internationally. I average 150,000-200,000 air miles a year. I have flown over 3,600,000   miles with American Airlines!

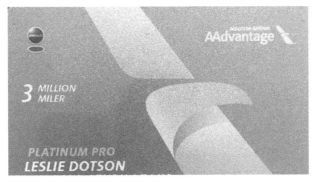

American Airlines 3.000,000 Miles Club

Whenever I fly, I always request the aisle seat; it allows me to be more attuned to every aspect of the plane and its passengers. Also, I prefer to be on the aisle because my legs are too long for the other seating options. I feel claustrophobic if I am on the window, and I feel like I am squished in the middle seat.

Since 911, whenever I travel, I make many observations in the airport terminal and really pay attention to what's going on with the flight and who's boarding. Before 911, I would just casually people watch. Now, I size up people in my mind and am always on the alert.

With so many flights, it's no wonder that I've encountered possible catastrophes every now and then and that my senses might detect danger, even before boarding. Once on the airplane and while in the air, they are always very keen.

CHAPTER 4

THE DISAPPEARING GUY

I usually fly first class when upgraded; it's more comfortable, plus I feel safer being closer to the captain. And engaging with people on flights seems to happen naturally. Usually, I sleep, read or do work, but in this particular instance, I was more than happy to introduce myself to the beautiful lady sitting in my row. But then we became involved in a mysterious incident, one that could have become a catastrophe. However, once again, I believe that my Angels were protecting me. *You be the judge…*

911 touched everyone around the world. It was a time that passengers on flights were checked, double-checked, and triple-checked. It was a time when everyone noticed and was alarmed and paranoid about any slight movement done wrong.

What a time, but it was an intense time of change, and checks and balances were needed for safety reasons with Airlines. *RIP the souls lost on the day of 911.*

My "Meeting" at 35,000 feet and the "Meaning" based on this post-911 scenario was one that I am sure saved lives, including mine. I, myself, got caught up at that tense time to start scanning the crowds of people in airports. I was consciously looking at anyone who seemed nervous or acted strangely while waiting for a flight, and observing 100 percent of the people on the flight itself.

I was on guard concerning anyone that got up too quickly to go to the bathroom, or started to argue with the flight attendants, or gave check-in people a hard time when they asked the security questions.

I was ready to do my civil duty, "DA" west side Carson style. All my peeps from home "la Raza" know precisely what this means. Peace ✌1

I was on a flight with colleagues heading from LAX to Hong Kong. Like any at that time, the flight was slow to board; there were double checks on everything. People were really concerned about security after 911. Everyone was starting to board and getting settled into the flight; boarding was just slow. I finally got to my row and was sitting in an aisle seat, and the window seat next to me was empty. I wished no one would sit next to me so I could have more space on this 15-hour flight to Hong Kong. Slowly coming down the aisle was a stunning woman…I mean, she was *gorgeous*… a supermodel for sure. I could see the guys ahead of me doing double-takes as she passed by their aisle…that is how beautiful she was. My colleagues in front of me, 10 rows up and across the aisle, were part of the crew of admirers, looking at her, as well.

Slowly, she approached my row. Then she stopped and looked at her ticket and then to the row numbers, and she said, "Hello, I am sitting next to you." I said, "Well, hello to you, as well." Then I got up and allowed her to enter into the window seat.

Across the way, I could see the guys looking back with pure envy, pointing, and obviously thinking, "You lucky dog. Holy shit, you are lucky!" I just laughed at them, got up, and walked over to them just to have a small chat. And of course, they were just talking all kinds of guy perverted s**t that we do, like little boys, as men. It was harmless and fun.

I went back to my seat while more people were boarding, and Miss America and I began the usual small conversation. I learned she was a runway supermodel and that she was on her way to Hong Kong to do a photoshoot. I wished her luck and congrats. She asked what I was going to Hong Kong for, and I told her about my design and manufacturing background in China. She was fascinated by this topic because she wanted to design a line of apparel / lingerie in China in the future. Of course, I told her I could help her in this direction and gave her my business card. She was grateful.

Now, here comes the turn of such a beautiful beginning of a flight boarding. *Beautiful model and everything!*

Remember, I told you that I was very caught up in scanning the people boarding the flights, and on the flights in the beginning. Well, I resumed my radar detecting *after* I was distracted by "Miss America"! (shining things have had such an effect on me, something I have learned to control over the years; thank goodness for those lessons learned in life!) More people were coming into the flight, and I noticed that one guy was holding a briefcase up to his chest with his two arms hugged around it. Now, you know my radar went off! *Why would he keep a briefcase in his arms like that when the case has a perfect handle on top of it to hold it with just one hand?* I was having red alarms going off. So, I zoned in on this guy as he walked down the aisle. It wasn't hot on the plane, but this guy was sweating! In fact, the AC was on while the people were boarding. *So, why was this guy sweating?* Foghorns started to go off in my head. He was very nervous about something.

The young lady next to me that I was just chatting to nicely could tell my disposition had changed, and she asked me if everything was all right. I whispered over to her and said, "Look at this guy with the briefcase coming down the aisle." She looked slowly down the aisle and saw him, and she said, just like me, "That is very strange." I said, "Right, how weird is this guy?" She said, "Yeah, he looks very nervous about something. Why is he holding that briefcase like that?"

You see, my universal red alarm horns were on the money. That is why, even today, many years later, after this incident, when my horns and sirens start to go off, I do not think it is just a *quinkidink*. Something is not *right*.

Back to the creepy guy. So, Miss America is now just as spooked as I am about this guy. She said, "Something is wrong with that guy; I can feel it." I said, "Me too." We both watched him as he approached our aisle and passed us. He sat behind us, maybe 2-3 rows back, cross side of our row in the last aisle seat next to the bathroom opening. I could see him out of the corner of my right eye if I turned my head just slightly to the right. Miss America said, "Can you see him?" I said, "Yes." She said, "What is he doing?" I said, "He is still holding the briefcase against his chest with two arms!" She goes, "No f***king way!" I said, "Yes f***king way, he is." She goes, "Oh shit! What should we do?" I said, "Nothing,.. let me just watch him." Eventually, after 2-3 minutes, he put the briefcase down in front of him, and he settled in. I told Miss America, "He settled down." And she said, "That is just   weird." I said, "Yes, I agree."

I told her that I would be right back. So, while people were still boarding, I went back to my colleagues to tell them what just happened. Once again, they were in front of me about 10 rows ahead and all the way to the right side of the plane. So, I made my way to the front and crossed over to talk to them. I got to their row and bent down to tell them softly what happened. It took me maybe 3-4 minutes to get to them, going through the people boarding and walking in the opposite direction. I was going upstream, and they were going downstream *like fish in a river.*

Once I told my colleagues what I saw, they peeped up their heads to look over the seats to see if they could see the guy I was talking about. They looked back and said, "We don't see a guy in that seat next to the bathroom on that aisle."

I looked back myself, and they were right; the guy wasn't there anymore. I thought that was strange. I told them, "I will be right back; I am going to check the bathroom." They said, "Okay, but be careful." As I crossed back over and started to go back down the aisle, I didn't see him. I could see Miss

America looking at me. I pointed at the empty seat, shrugged my shoulders, and placed my hands up, like a question of, *where did he go?*. I got down the aisle, passed my seat area, and went to his row. The briefcase was there on the floor, propped up against the chair, but he was not there.

I went to check the bathrooms that were by his seat. Both of the latches were in the green position, not red, indicating that no one was in either bathroom. *Strange,* I thought. I went further back past the bathrooms, and there was only one more sizeable section of the mid to back of the plane. So, I scanned this area, but I still didn't see him. I thought, *maybe like me, he went to visit a friend or family member in the back of the plane.* In the front of my section was first class; I didn't think that he would go that way, and I didn't notice that he passed me when I was visiting my colleagues. So, I went back to my seat feeling puzzled. I asked Miss America if she saw him pass by. She said, "No." So, we both thought he probably went to the back bathrooms for some reason.

The final people boarded the plane, and the flight attendants started to do their customary pre-takeoff rituals. Miss America and I were now very concerned that after about another 5 minutes had gone by and he hadn't returned to his seat. We said to each other, "Okay, something is wrong." *He hadn't come back to the seat even as the plane was in final preparation.*

At this point, I decided to ring my call button. The flight attendant came to our aisle and said, "Can I help you, sir?" I said, "Yes, you can." I started to explain that a guy was sitting in that seat, and now he is no longer there. My colleagues saw me speaking to the flight attendant and came over to assist. The flight attendant took the situation very seriously, and she immediately called the Air Marshals on the flight. They arrived quickly, and she explained the situation to them. Then, the Air Marshals started asking people sitting next to the empty seat if they knew who was sitting there. The people told them no, and stated that they were not related. They just saw the man sit down, then get up and leave. The air marshals asked which way he went. The lady who'd been sitting next to him said she didn't pay attention because she was facing her husband and getting settled in. When she turned around, he was gone. She said that she was sorry that she couldn't help.

The captain came back, and they immediately got the flight roster to check the passenger's name. The Air Marshall directed everyone that was sitting in the area not to move. One by one, they had people verify who they were with the name on the roster. Everyone checked out okay. They sent Air Marshals to the back of the plane to check the bathroom. By then, everyone was watching. The strange man was still nowhere to be found. They checked all the rows, one by one. Nothing. He wasn't there. Finally, they went on the intercom and stated his name and said he should present himself if he was on board. There was no response. He literally disappeared off the plane.

The Air Marshal then decided he needed to react fast. He moved everyone back, and then he decided on his own to remove the briefcase! He picked it up slowly with gloves and immediately took it off the plane. *Fast.* I do not think they had procedures to deal with this kind of situation then. Now I believe they deplane everyone and call in the bomb units to remove these unaccompanied packages or cases.

The captain went back up front and then came on the intercom and explained the situation; they had to un-board a suitcase on the plane as well and redo the safety check.

The Air Marshal and Flight Attendants came over. They thanked us for saying something, as it was a very unusual situation. It was better to be safe than sorry. We agreed, as well.

They never said what happened to the guy and or the briefcase after we landed. For me, I didn't want to know. I was just glad he and his briefcase were off the flight. We were still nervous the whole flight to Hong Kong.

The "Meaning" of this story is to be a good citizen and to recognize these types of situations. Who knows what was in the briefcase and what this creepy guy was up to? And the souls on that flight didn't want to know either, as it became a conversation during the flight with people. *Did we save a potential incident?* Only the Universe knows. We are safe and sound, and that is all that matters in the end.

Stay gone, Disappearing Guy, no one wants to know your "Meaning" at 35,000 Feet! The "Meeting" was safe and sound. Peace ✌

CHAPTER 5

GIVING BACK
TO MY FELLOW MAN

Being able to give back to humanity gives me the most joy in my life. I love any opportunity to be involved in some type of charity event, give-back program, or some type of holistic healing program. I firmly believe that is my calling. Working and contributing in a charitable or holistic environment gives me joy and peace in my heart. It's something that I have been wanting to do, and I am now driven towards it because it has become my passion.

When I am "serving" or giving back, I either do public speaking at a men's group or donate things to people or participate in a special event. Whenever my time permits, I also go to the homeless shelter and help out there. I talk to the people and in some way bond with them, by giving advice and helping them to look to the future in a good way. The meaning of these meetings is always revealed to me at some point, just as when I am flying,

Gardena CA, Boys and Girls Club giving away backpacks
I had in storage for Christmas 2019

One of the organizations that I belong to is Sacred Sons, a 3-year-old men's group with members from all over the world - Germany, Italy, Taiwan, and Canada, just to name a few. We are brothers, fathers, husbands, and uncles, and our membership is still growing strong, with many women helping to spread the word. Talking to fellow members at the men's group meetings is enlightening. We discuss life issues - children, pain, relationships, everything, freely expressing ourselves with our "brothers".

A safe container for warriors to come and shed the trama and heal the pain in good spirit.

All are welcome no matter your creed or background.
www.sacredsons.com

We are here to help each other heal and awaken our authentic power through participation in circles, workshops, retreats, and online courses. Drawing upon ancient wisdom and modern technologies of human development, the leaders utilize the power of ceremony, ritual, and intentional spaces to deepen into authentic brotherhood and catalyze growth in men. Through time-tested frameworks and psychological processes, Sacred Sons guides men to their emotional and spiritual edges. Every man who shows up and does the inner work will one day feel the full depth and breadth of his emotions, find and honor his purpose in life, and commit to embodying his truth.

I wholeheartedly believe that my involvement with Sacred Sons has helped me be more open to my friends' needs and given me the ability to invite new friends into my inner circle. I am susceptible, especially when I travel, because I never know who I will be sitting next to.

With this newly developed awareness of self, I seem to draw people to me that have a purpose in my life. Some may become business associates. Others may develop a bond or a lifetime friendship; sometimes they may need my advice, and sometimes I may need theirs. Whatever the connection may turn out to be, I believe it is because I am spiritual, aware, and connected to the universe.

Brothers helping another Brother move the trauma away.

Below, I have included 7 fundamental principles that the Sacred Sons share with their members as they journey to find their purpose. They are referred to as PILLARS OF SACRED SONS:

1. Brotherhood: We stand as an inclusive community of brothers seeking to end the lone wolf and to co-steward the return of the father archetype on this planet. We rise together!

2. Accountability: We are committed to aligning and re-aligning the integrity of ourselves and other men when agreements and responsibilities have been broken. We support each brother to take action from truth and accountability.

3. InterSovereignty: We acknowledge the part within oneself that recognizes the part within another, knowing we are whole, loving, and unfuckwithable.

4. Authenticity: We honor and recognize each brother as a unique being, embracing his individual path and showing up for himself and the people in his life without judgment.

5. Listening: We are here to witness and listen to others' truths, stories, and impacts from an embodied masculine archetype.

6. Acceptance: We recognize the value of accepting ourselves and others as we are through holding the awareness of collective love and letting go of control.

7. Vulnerability: We recognize that we create the space for others to be open and vulnerable from a place of empowerment by doing our own inner-work.

*Our own Ocean 4-5 at my 50Th Birthday Party
and Wedding Best Men*

CHAPTER 6

FRIEND IN NEED IN
THE UNIVERSE

Scan QR code with phone
To See Chapter Preview

I know I am connected to the Universe by vibration, by timing, and just by sheer will. Two or three of my friends and I see each other outside of the United States more often than inside or their own country. The timing is just amazing, without planning and just "meeting" by chance. It's as if we are traveling lights that connect when the frequency is just right.

I have one great brother friend who has platinum wings... more than I do. He is 100 percent a global traveler and has many stories of his own.

Two different meetings are unique between him and me that I will never forget.

One was our first "meeting". I was on my way to Brazil with a dual connection flight from Los Angeles to Miami and then Miami to Rio de Janeiro. The flight was packed, and the majority of the passengers were Brazilians. I scanned the crowd of people as I usually do before boarding a plane; the diversity of the people all on the same flight fascinated me. I really like it when there are babies on the flight, as it reinsures my heart in a way that the flight will be safe - just my own gut feeling. I smile when I see the little ones. Most people don't, though, worried that they'll have to sit next to the babies, who will cry on the flight. For me, however, I am happy the children are there.

As I scanned the crowd, I noticed another business "brother" out of the many passengers. He was dressed in semi-business attire, and I was curious about his reason for going to Rio. *Was it for business or pleasure?* As we boarded the flight, it was a slow process.

When I came to my seat, the same "brother" that I noticed outside the flight was coincidently sitting next to me in the same aisle, on the two-seater side of the plane.

Let the "Meeting" begin.

When two "brothers" meet while traveling, we always wonder what the purpose of the travel is, where we come from, what our backgrounds are, and how the families and relationships in our business and personal lives are. It is incredible, at least in my years of travel, the level of conversations I have when sitting next to someone of the same ethnicity.

This brother, Benson, had the same background in global travels, sales, product development, marketing, and presence in a world that is so far away from us. It was refreshing to see another brother - from the same neck of the woods in Los Angeles - go through the same trials and tribulations in life as I have. We both understood that those occurrences were necessary to learn and grow from.

That "Meeting" validated my life pattern, and the results of those life patterns came from experiencing the same flow. Both of us were amazed by the synergy. It was just a true blessing. The flight was six hours, and Benson and I must have compared notes on every subject. We talked in-depth about the women in our lives, our trippy life experiences, our beautiful children, fatherhood, our families, our struggles with society as a whole, politics in the USA, and why so many people are moving to other countries to retire. We discussed travel in general and the many experiences in the travels - both funny, sad and surprising. When Benson and I landed in Rio, since this was his first time there, we connected with my local Brazilian friends. All of us became very close friends and, of course, we had a wonderful time with locals and the beauty that Rio can provide! (We know the meaning of these meetings ©)

Ironically, four to five times in our many travels abroad, Benson and I were either in the same country or the same city at the same time, unplanned. It was a fantastic connection to have with a fellow traveler and remarkable how the universe syncs our existences.

It proved this connection again on this particular journey, five years after Benson and I met.

Three weeks before one of my regular trips to China, I heard from my co-universal travel buddy, Benson. Apparently, he was headed to India to check out some new manufacturing locations. There was no planned connection with him at all in our travel schedules.

Once in China, *I must have gone to about 5 providences in 10 days.* Then I had a departing flight out of Hong Kong back to LAX direct.

I went to the First-class lounge, did some same-day shopping, and waited while people went through pre-boarding processes. I was on the phone having a follow-up conversation with clients and business partners before catching the 11-hour direct flight back to LAX.

The next thing I knew, I felt a tap on my right shoulder from behind. It startled me for a moment because I was speaking to someone on the phone. When I turned around to see who or what was tapping me on the shoulder, to my damn surprise, it was my fellow traveling brother, Benson!

I told the person on the phone to let me call them back because I was surprised as hell to see Benson in the airport catching the same flight me! He said that when he scanned the crowd, as I do, he noticed from behind that it was me. He was just amazed to see me and came over to surprise me.

I said, "Bro, what the hell is this? Of all places in the world, why would the universe put us back together on the same flight, just like when we first met?"

The Second "Meeting" begins!

Again, Benson and I could not believe the synergy. *How could it be possible that we are on the same flight, unplanned?* There had to be a divine connection. We probed our travel schedules from the last 2-3 weeks, and there was no connection. We both headed to Hong Kong from opposite directions. He was in India, then he went to Thailand, and then to Hong Kong.

I was in China and then in Hong Kong. We both changed our Hong Kong flight days and times and then still ended up on the same flight.

Why? What was the "Meaning"? Benson and I both know without a doubt that we are connected by the divine universe. We are here for each other in times of need, to help each other or just to listen to life's trials and tribulations.

At that time, Benson had a big problem in his life. He needed a brother, a dear friend, to be there for him in his time of need. It was one of those problems in life that needed no blame, judgment, or 'I told you so'. He just needed a confidant to share his thoughts and feelings of how he planned to deal with this situation when he got back to Los Angeles.

Benson would have been driving himself crazy on that eleven hour flight back to Los Angeles had he been alone. The universe didn't allow that; it placed us on the same flight at "35,000" feet to have a "Meeting". The "Meaning" of that "Meeting" was to be the 'soldier' for my brother, to hear him, be that rock of peace, and provide the salvation of brother ship that we lack today in this world among men. What he needed was the feminine in the masculine. There was no puffed-up chest, no warrior boundaries or knives of wisdom. Our meeting was a time of gentle listening - a time to console, pray for a positive outcome, and allow this   broken man to be held in the space of compassion.

After 11 hours of talking back and forth during the flight, Benson landed well in Los Angeles. He was ready to face his tribulations, well-armed with good guidance and a perspective on handling the situation. Months later, the problem was resolved. He transcended well, lesson learned.

Benson and I will never forget this "Meeting" at 35.000 feet and its "Meaning". Love and peace, my brother. Love and peace.

CHAPTER 7

RESPONSIBLE ADULTS

When I was young, everyone was partying, getting drunk, doing drugs, and all kinds of craziness. It was the thing to do because it was "cool" back in the 80s and 90s. But that was a different time. Now, in 2020 we are all responsible adults, and we know that getting high or drunk is not the way to socialize anymore.

I saw how that lifestyle hurt my friends; people were getting in car accidents and injuring people or being violent with each other. Marriages were broken up. So, I just said, "You know, really, guys! I don't need that kind of stuff around."

Now, everyone I am around or associate with drinks responsibly, so I would say they are very light social drinkers. My friends know they need to be sober around their families; they'll take an Uber if they decide to go out. I don't have anyone around me who is drunk, falling out, or belligerent.

When I do drink, it is usually only beer or wine. *But my favorite drink is called a Madras – it's orange, cranberry, and Grey Goose Vodka on the rocks.*

My ex-wife even asked me, "Les, why don't you have any partying friends?" I told her, "I stopped going over to those kinds of people's houses a long time ago. It's just not worth it. There's too much trouble, too much drama, and I just don't want to deal with that." I'd rather be in peace and quiet and tranquility and be on a high vibration. I just don't want to deal with it anymore. I did that when I was young.

I never found myself passed out because I was always the designated driver, the responsible one, always getting us home. But, that's what happens to many girls when they go out with "predators". For one reason or another, they pass out, and these guys take advantage of them. Then, it's his word against her word.

Because I have seen so many things and heard so many stories, I become particularly annoyed when I am in an environment where people are loud and falling out drunk. So, you can imagine how close I had come to my boiling point when I encountered "Crazy Patricia" during a "Meeting" at 35,000 feet.

CHAPTER 8

CRAZY PATRICIA

Now that you know how I feel about people drinking too much, this should give you quite a chuckle. All I can say is wow… what a "Meeting" in the sky. To this day, I am still trying to figure out the "Meaning" of *this* "Meeting".

I took a Redeye flight from LAX to Bradley, 9:15 pm to 5:30 am. I tried my best to get an upgrade because I really needed to get some sleep. I was tired and wanted to rest and be ready for the next few days on the east coast. It was 'no go' on the upgrade, but at least I got the Bulkhead aisle, seat 7C. At least, at the time, that is what I thought was my lucky number 7. Anyone who knows me knows that 7 is a very good number for me; 7-7-17 was my wedding day celebration, for example, Boeing 777, etc.

The flight was 100% booked, and people were slow on this particular evening to get to their seats. I reached my "lucky 7" aisle seat and started to get settled in. I could see that the people around to my left had their head pillows positioned and were snuggled in their jackets. .. Behind me, one girl was in pajama-like clothes with woolly boots and a hoody over her head. *She was fully ready to get some ZZZZz.* Then next to me, in seats 7B and 7A, there was a couple.

Next to me was a cowboy; he had a nice cowboy hat, blue jeans and cowboy boots, and a plaid print design. He was an older gentleman but very distinguished-looking, and he had presence. I could also faintly smell some type of alcohol coming from his pores – bourbon or whiskey - so he must have gotten a couple of drinks before boarding the plane. He looked over at me, tipped his hat, and said, "Hello, my name is Tom." I said hello back, shook his hand, and said, "My name is Les; nice to meet you."

Tom and I started to have the usual small chat while getting settled into our seats, such as: where are you from, where are you going, and why are we taking the red-eye, are we crazy, etc., etc.… He seemed to be a very nice guy, full of life, and pleasant.

A woman was sitting kind of close to Tom, and he was chatting with her in small talk… I assumed it was his wife. After five minutes or so of Tom and me chitchatting, his wife, at least who I believed her to be at the time, leaned forward to make sure I saw her. She looked at me with a strange but opening look, the look that is like, *"Hey, I want to tell you something,"* kind of look people can give you sometimes. Then, she said slowly and very loud, "Hey Les, Hi…" I said, "Hi…" Then she said, in the same slow, loud voice (so loudly that the people to my right and behind me could hear her), "I just wanted to let you know before we take off, I AM CRAZY! My name is Patricia, and Yes, I AM CRAZY! I just wanted to let you know before we took off, Ok?!"

When I heard this, the first thing that popped into my mind was that this lady is just joking because she was sitting right next to her husband. He can hear her and the people behind me, and to the right could hear her. Before I responded at all, I did a quick scan to see if they had, and all the people to the right of me had that look on their face like, 'Oh shit, here we go'. The girl behind me in PJs just shook her head, with a 'is this for real' expression on her face.

I looked at Tom, sitting next to me, and he started to turn a little pinkish-red of embarrassment. But, since Crazy Patricia was speaking directly to me, I felt compelled to respond… so, I did. "Well, that is nice to know, Patricia, before we take off… thanks for the warning. She cracked a wicked weird smile at me and said, "Well, I thought it was only fair to let you know before we took off, Les… Now you know." I said to myself, o*h boy, this lady is crazy;* I never heard anyone admit, with such calm demeanor, that she is crazy to everyone around her.

Once again, she started to speak in a loud voice, leaning forward and looking directly at me, asking questions, "Les! Hi Les! Where are you going???" I answered slowly because, at that point, I was highly concerned about what information to give to this lady… I said, "Connecticut". She said even louder, ME TOO! Then I realized the alcohol smell was coming from her, more than Tom!

At this point, I really tried my best to prepare to get some sleep, as I knew there was going to be a long day ahead of me...

But Patricia had no consideration of the loudness of her voice. When she spoke, it was at top volume. I was sure the people behind us could hear everything she was saying. Finally, the Flight attendant came over and asked her to please speak more softly. Patricia replied, "Oh, I am sorry, am I speaking too loud?!" I thought to myself, *this lady really has no clue of her presence.*

Before the flight took off, Patricia asked for a drink for the second time, and the Flight attendant told her that she would have to wait for the beverage service. I thought that this lady already had enough drinks, and giving her more would just make it worse!

So here we go... We take off, and the flight is smooth. Patricia is still speaking loudly to Tom while everyone is trying to sleep, and poor Tom is doing his best to quiet her. The beverage service begins, and she orders a double Jack Daniels! Tom is asking her constantly to lower her voice. . She would, for a moment, then say sorry repeatedly - but went right back to the loud volume voice. The people to the left of me and behind me were very annoyed at this point, and I can see that they are not happy at all in their faces. They implore the Flight Attendant, again, to tell Patricia to keep her voice down.

Once again, Patricia acknowledges and then goes right back to "the outdoor voice". The young lady behind us in the PJs had enough; she sat up and pulled back Patricia's seat and told her, "Shut the hell up! You are making too much noise, and people are trying to sleep on this red-eye, lady!" Patricia just looked at her, and went right back to repeatedly apologizing to Tom. At that point, I looked at Tom in disbelief. He shrugged his shoulders in despair.

The flight attendant came back through to refresh people's drinks and pick up trash; once again, Patricia ordered another double of Jack Daniels!

I got up to go to the bathroom, and Patricia said super loudly, "HEY LES, WHERE ARE YOU GOING?" I couldn't believe it. The whole front section of the plane awoke and was super pissed off, making all kinds of comments and gestures to this lady. I said to her, "To the bathroom, and you need to be quieter Patricia; you are disturbing people." She said, in a soft kid's voice, "Okay Les, you are right, I will be quieter." Then she said in a louder voice, looking back at the people in the front section of the plane, "SORRY! I will be better... I will be quieter... now that I have my drinks!"

When I went to the bathroom, the Flight Attendants stopped me and repeatedly apologized for the situation. I just said to them, "Please do not give that lady anything else to drink... It is clear, guys, this lady has a problem, and alcohol is just making it worse for all of us!" They said, "Oh, she is 100% cut off." They explained there was nothing more they could do because the flight was full, and we were in mid-air.

I came back from the bathroom, and Patricia was looking right at me. She shouted, "Hi Les, you are back. Is everything ok? We missed you!" I couldn't believe this lady... Really...

I sat down, put a blanket over my back, and turned my back to both of them to try to get some sleep through their conversations. I could clearly hear, unfortunately, that these two were not married after all. Patricia had two kids in Los Angeles, and Tom was on a business trip; they met each other at the airport bar.

It was crazy. Patricia found out that Tom was going through a divorce and she started to accuse him of cheating on her, already! Tom was saying, "Hey, we just met." Patricia said, "you are just like all the other men, cheating on me." After that, she asked Tom twice to come back to her place when they landed, and Tom tried to explain to her that he was headed in the other direction of Connecticut. She tried to convince him of why he should come with her and not go to his house. I couldn't believe these two were actually having this conversation that everyone could hear. Tom should have just shut up, but he was getting pulled into the conversation even more.

The next thing I knew, these two started making out on the plane... I mean full-on making out; it was f**king crazy... I have never witnessed two people who just met each other, one clearly crazy and the other, engaging in such an act. I tried my best to turn my back to this energy. *It was the most uncomfortable "meeting" on a plane I have ever experienced...*

Four hours later, the plane landed, and everyone was super annoyed, pissed, and wanted to kill this lady. You could feel the tension in the air when everyone stood up to collect their belongings. Patricia told Tom, "Hey, by the way, my name is not Patricia, my name is Rebecca! Nice to meet you." Meanwhile, everyone who was standing watched with dismay. People started to file out of the plane, and then Patricia turned to me and said, "Hey Les... SO nice to meet you... It was a pleasure to know you... Tom and I are going to go home now... Sorry for the loud talking... you take care now and see you later." Then she walked out of the plane with bloodshot eyes, reeking of Jack Daniels and stumbling down the jetway.

Once again, I have to tell you I have no idea of the "meaning" of this "meeting", but it is an experience I will never forget in my life... Crazy Patricia, *I mean Rebecca...*

Needless to say, I am a people person. Every day is something totally different; you never know what's going to happen next. I pride myself on knowing how to observe and communicate with people in a positive way....but this one took the prize... Crazy Patricia totally stumped me... that's something to think about, something to ponder. I'm sure, one day, I will realize the "meaning" of that "meeting".

CHAPTER 9

BE TRUE TO YOURSELF

So, I must say to you that I have learned to love ALL people of all persuasions and ethnicities in this world, and I understand that we all have specific attractions. However, when it comes to sexual orientations, I am compelled to say that it's important to "Stay in Your Lane." There is no need to create discomfort or uneasiness by making suggestions or "hitting on" someone who is obviously not swinging your way. That being said, I hope you enjoy my next "Meeting" in Chapter 10. Here is a good lead in to the next chapter:

As Ralph Waldo Emerson (1803-1882), the American essayist, lecturer, philosopher, poet, champion of individualism and opponent of conformity, put it so well, "To be yourself in a world that is constantly trying to make you something else is the *greatest* accomplishment."

For gay men/women, learning to accept their "different" sexual orientation as a positive aspect of themselves is only part of their "coming out." For all men and women, regardless of sexual orientation, the more significant challenge is to embrace the things about ourselves that make us unique.

Henry "Harry" Hay Jr. (April 7, 1912 – October 24, 2002) was a prominent American gay rights activist, communist, and labor advocate. He was a founder of the Mattachine Society, the first sustained gay rights group in the United States, and the Radical Faeries, a loosely affiliated gay spiritual movement.

Hay is generally acknowledged as the contemporary "father of gay liberation" and coined terms such as the gay window, subject-subject consciousness, and a separate people whose time has come. Hay held forth the idea that gay people and their sexuality embody a form of consciousness different from the mainstream, and believed that they have a unique contribution to humanity. However, he stressed that gay people must determine for themselves what this perspective might be.

Enjoy the next chapter on my "Meeting" at 35.000 feet on this subject matter.

CHAPTER 10

YOU ARE CUTE

A "Meeting" of diversity at 35,000 feet. "You Are Cute," and its "Meanings" are still controversial today. I have literally encountered all human races, creeds, cultures, religions and sexual preferences.

In this "Meeting" at 35,000 feet, I was confronted with two of our brothers on the gay side working as flight attendants. One was working in the front of the plane and the other in the back. To clarify, I am a straight brother, love my women, and am not on the DL. But I wanted to tell this story, as it has great meaning in our society today.

On my way to a business meeting in NY from LA, I was well-dressed in my business fashion attire. It's just how I roll. *Thanks, Dad, for teaching me how to dress like a gentleman.*

When I boarded the plane, there were two gents greeting people onto the plane. Both brothers were well-groomed, well-spoken, and helpful to the people. When I stepped onto the plane, one of the guys hit the other guy's arm to get his attention. The other one looked my way, and I immediately saw what was going on. One of them said, "Well, hello, Mr. Man", and the other said, "I see you are well today." The other passengers near me paused for a moment; they also got   the gist of what was up. A couple of the ladies in front of me gave a little laugh.

I said, "Yo, what's up, all is good," in my NY accent (living in NY for 8 years rubbed off on me), and I gave them a peace-up sign and head nod, with force to let them know I am straight.

I am sure they got the point, but these two gents had their own force and agenda. I take it this was not the first time they encountered passengers of choice to hit on because they were in sync with their gestures. One of them said, "I got you, Mr. Man, no worries… we will take care of you." Then he said something under his breath that I couldn't hear.

I got settled in my seat on the aisle. On this flight, there was no upgrade, but an exit row seat is just fine with me. Everyone got settled down, and the flight attendants were preparing to take off by giving the safety speech and video. One of the flight attendants by the door came by my exit row and began the safety procedure with the equipment. He kept looking at me while he was doing the procedure. It's funny-when the flight attendants do this process, they usually have a blank stare on their faces and look straight down the aisle of the plane. However, this guy was making an obvious expression towards me. I checked around me to see if others were noticing, and the lady next to me was looking at him as well. I think she could see that he kept looking over our way.

After he finished, he wrapped up the equipment and placed it back into the overhead. The lady next to me leaned over and whispered, "I think that guy likes you," with a giggle in her voice. I looked at her with a semi-serious face and told her, "I don't roll that way." She said, "I don't think this guy cares how you roll," and then she laughed.

Now look, I have been around many gay brothers and sisters through my entire life. We grew up with a clear understanding of the opposite sex and same-sex relationships. It has just been a part of our lives, in our family, high school and college, and in the workforce globally.

My personal thoughts and beliefs are *"to each their own"*. Whatever a person feels internally or has learned to be in their relationships is their journey in life. Yes, as a Christian, I have been brought that same-sex relationships are different. The Bible in Romans 1-2 identifies the biblical belief, which you can read and interpret for yourself.

It also says to "love your neighbor, honor them in all aspects of life, and to pray for those (and myself) WHO SIN." I believe that no SIN is any less or any greater and that Jesus Christ came here as a n example for us. Sins have always been here and will always be. Because He died for our sins, we are to be forgiven through repentance and prayer.

In the end, all is love, no matter your sexual preference. So again, to each their own.

"Love is patient and kind, never jealous, boastful, proud, or rude. Love isn't selfish or quick-tempered. It doesn't keep a record of wrongs that others do. Love rejoices in the truth, but not in evil. Love is always supportive, loyal, hopeful, and trusting." Love Never Fails. (1 Corinthians 13:4-7 CEVDCI) https://www.bible.com/303/1co.13.4-7.cevdci

Now that the seriousness is over let's get back to the story because it gets very interesting. As this flight attendant started to walk to the back of the plane, he stopped by my seat and said, "Mr. Dotson, I see that you are an Executive Plat with 3 million miles. Congratulations! If you need anything, just let me know. I am here to serve you."

The lady next to me just started busting up laughing when he left the area and bumped my shoulder. She said, "I told you so."

I said, "He is just being nice. He has to say that." She said, "Yeah, right! I'm an Exec Plat too, and he didn't say anything to me, doesn't know my name or miles status." She continued laughing. I said, "HaHaHa, very funny!"

All through the first 3.5 hours of the flight, these two guys kept coming back and forth; and every time they came by my seat aisle, they stopped and asked if I wanted something or was there anything they could do. By the 4th time, I felt really uncomfortable, mainly because the lady next to me was getting such a kick out of it the entire time.

I needed to use the restroom, so I unbuckled and started to head to the back of the plane. When I was halfway there, one of the guys looked at me and literally did the following:

He spread his arms to the top of the plane ceiling and spread his legs aisle to aisle, and said, "If you want to use these bathrooms, you are going to have to go through me!"

Now I was just shocked. I didn't know if this guy was serious or playing a joke to f**k with me further. Now look, I am not an a**hole, and I am not angered easily, but I just didn't know if this guy was kidding. So, I said, "Look, brother, I've got to go to the bathroom, and that is very funny, but I gotta go."

He said, "Well, you are going to have to go through me to get there", and he stood his ground even more seriously with this quirky look on his face. "Yes, I've been watching you, ever since you got on this plane, with your cute little self, and you are going to talk to me."

I said, "Ok brother, look, I don't roll that way. I am straight up."

He said, "That's what they all say."

I said, "Brother, seriously, I've got to go to the bathroom." Luckily for me, another passenger behind me also got up to use the bathroom, so he let down his "human body barricade" to the bathroom. I quickly moved towards him, and he let me by, but kept staring at me the whole time. I didn't know whether to be offended or angry. As I came out of the bathroom, he said, "I was just playing you, boy. Don't take it so seriously."

I said, "I am not." I gave him a nod and strolled back to my seat. For the rest of the flight, I didn't get up. I stayed right there. They both continued to give these slight looks and small comments as they went by my seat. The lady next to me was still enjoying every time they passed by. I just tried to ignore them. It wasn't worth the trouble. They knew I was straight, and they just wanted to make me feel uncomfortable. I didn't let it bother me.

In the end, the flight landed, and we deplaned. When I got to the front door, one of the guys was there. He said, "Nice flying with you, Mr. Dotson. The pleasure has been all mine." I just said "thanks" and moved past him as quickly as possible.

Now look, I know this sounds funny, but it was uncomfortable. I guess it's the same as a man hitting on a woman or a woman hitting on a man in a flight. It was weird, but I didn't let it get me angry or upset. I chalked it up as an experience of life, and, once again, people have their own preferences. In the end, though, we should all respect and honor each other's space and have love and peace as humans.

The key and "meaning" to this story is people will do what they want to do with their lives, and we all need to honor what we believe. Don't try to change people and allow them to live their karma path.

But, please - leave the pathway to the bathroom clear on a flight!

Peace. Namaste.

CHAPTER 11

IT'S NICE TO BE KIND

Love is patient; love is kind.
-1 Corinthians 13:4

WORDS RELATED TO KIND are: sympathetic, affectionate, charitable, amiable, kindly, kindhearted, cordial, courteous, compassionate, tolerant, thoughtful, humane, gracious, considerate, friendly, loving.

Often we use the terms nice and kind in the same sentence. We describe people as nice and kind interchangeably. I believe that there is an important difference between the two and that, while it is nice to be nice, it is essential to be kind.
– Owen Fitzpatrick

Being nice is when you are polite to people and treat people well. Being kind is when you care about people and show you care. Sometimes you can be kind to someone, even though you aren't nice to them and you can certainly be nice to someone, but also be unkind.

You cannot be taught to be kind. Being kind comes from caring enough for others so that you want to do something for them. One of the hardest yet most important things we must learn to do is start being kind to everyone we can.

Obviously, there may be certain exceptions, such as those who have harmed you or your loved ones. But I believe that most people need our kindness, regardless of their race, creed, religion, culture, sexual preference, or social status... We must start to care more about others and seek to help them in more ways. Not because we should, or because it is how we want to be seen, but because being kind is fundamentally the greatest gift we can give to the world.

It is easy to be nice. It is easy to plaster on a smile and treat people respectfully, but being kind is a different matter. Being kind requires that we look at others and treat others with genuine consideration. Kindness requires that we allow ourselves to see ourselves in them and connect with them as human beings. Lastly, kindness requires that we work to help others have a better life.

Be kind to one another is my suggestion.

> *Be kind and compassionate to one another, forgiving each other, just as in Christ, God forgave you.* **- Ephesians 4:32 NIV**

> *But love your enemies, do good to them, and lend to them without expecting to get anything back. Then your reward will be great, and you will be children of the Most High, because He is kind to the ungrateful and wicked.* **- Luke 6:35 NIV**

Those who are kind benefit themselves, but the cruel bring ruin on themselves. **- Proverbs 11:17 NIV**

Therefore, as God's chosen people, holy and dearly loved, clothe yourselves with compassion, kindness, humility, gentleness, and patience. **- Colossians 3:12 NIV**

Love is patient; love is kind. It does not envy, it does not boast, it is not proud. It does not dishonor others, it is not self-seeking, it is not easily angered, it keeps no record of wrongs. **- 1 Corinthians 13:4-5 NIV**

Therefore, as we have opportunity, let us do good to all people, especially to those who belong to the family of believers. **- Galatians 6:10 NIV**

Do not repay evil with evil or insult with insult. On the contrary, repay evil with blessing, because to this you were called so that you may inherit a blessing. **- 1 Peter 3:9 NIV**

Blessed are the merciful, for they will be shown mercy. **- Matthew 5:7 NIV**

CHAPTER 12

MS. DANCER

"Ms. Dancer", a first-class flight attendant. "Meeting" at 35,000 feet; "Meaning" of life change.

I am going to make this story short and sweet, and to the point. This "Meeting" was, once again, of the divine.

The "Meaning" was apparent to me. "Do good unto others as others do good unto you."

There is a big difference, I think, between being "kind" and being "nice". "Kind" asks for nothing in return and has no agenda; the results are pure. "Nice" usually has some type of exchange of service or want and desire between people. Sometimes, it's even manipulative.

In this case, I was purely "kind", and the circumstances of the actual event were in a place where "kind" was just not heard of.

I was flying from LAX to Dubai. I had a stop in Qatar and then on to Dubai. On my flight, I had the biggest surprise that I could have imagined. I got upgraded to first-class (thank you again), and I settled into the flight. Away we went. During the dinner service, I noticed one of the flight attendants on the other side of the aisle. Something about her caught my eye. She looked Romanian or Bulgarian. It kept bugging me and bugging me. I kept saying to myself, *I know this lady. I have seen her somewhere before.* I kept wondering, *on what flight have I seen her before?* I started scrolling through my mind about the various international fights I had taken. But, nothing was coming to my mind.

So, later during the flight, I decided to go to the bathroom before I did my yoga routine, and I saw her coming through the galley. Once again, it was bugging me like crazy. *I know this lady.* So, I stopped what I was doing, and I went over to her and said, "Hello. How are you?"

I could see from the look on her face that she also recognized me, and she said, "Oh my God, it *is* you". At first, I was surprised because I still couldn't figure out where I knew her from, but I knew clearly at that moment I had seen or spoken with her before.

She asked, "You don't remember me, do you?" I said, "I am sorry, I cannot figure it out." She said, "I will never forget you." Now I am thinking, *oh s**t, did I sleep with this girl in my "dark" days and not remember? Sorry, mom, that happens…when we're young.*

She knew by the look on my face that I couldn't pull it together. Then, she came near me, pulled me close, and whispered in my ear so others couldn't hear her. She told me…!

I said, "Ahh, now I remember." *Are you ready, readers?* She was a dancer in a gentlemen's club in Florida, which I went to many years ago. That is where I met her… Almost about 15 years before this flight...

I couldn't believe running into her on a flight to Qatar, of all places, and at 35,000 feet. Now, you know she and I were trippin'. She pulled me aside and said, "How are you?" I said, "How are *you?*" She told me her new life was *wonderful*. She said again, "I will never forget you." I asked, "Why?" She explained, "You were very *kind* to me at a time in my life when I was in a very dark place."

I told her, "Yes, I remember now. We had a long talk about choices in life, and how we make them can change our life path forever." She said, "You left such an impression on me that I took our conversation to heart and decided the following week to make better choices for myself. I chose to get out of that line of work and to do something interesting and different."

After a few job changes to build her resume and build history, she told me that she applied to be a flight attendant and got the job!!! Now she travels worldwide and is seeing things that she never thought she would experience in life. She said, "It was because you were *kind* and talked to me like a true human being and didn't want anything else from me but to talk. And now, here you are in front of me, on my dream job, and I get to thank you!"

It was a moment of pure gratefulness. A moment of the true divine. *Kind. Just be kind.* It can change people's lives for the better.

We hugged each other, exchanged numbers, and I thanked her. She said, "No, I thank *you* for being *kind* to me; it helped me to change my life karma."

God and the universe can work in mysterious ways for the good in everything.

Keep being Kind. Keep the spirit alive in your heart versus your mind. Quiet the Ego and have discernment, of course, as this is the balance

I loved this 'Meeting" at 35,000 feet because the "Meaning" showed our true purpose in life.

Peace and love to you. Fly girl, fly.

Besos, Les.

CHAPTER 13

THE CREATIVE MIND
VS THE HEART

A gentleman was teaching a class that I attended about the creative mind vs. the heart. He shared a study that I found absolutely fascinating. The study stated, "The heart that we have inside of us can feel and react to a situation even before the mind does." And when I saw the study, I thought, *OMG, I know how that feels.* I can always base my judgment of a person on how my heart feels - sometimes my heart says, "Wow, I want to know this person more!" And if there is something strange about something or weird about somebody, my heart feels it, and I want to be distanced from this person. The whole feeling of that particular encounter comes into my mind, and it's usually 99% accurate... felt just by my heart.

When traveling, the conversations just seem to happen by themselves, and when they do, it's like a magical connection. Other flights are just totally silent with no interaction. I am not over-friendly, but when drawn to someone, I have a connection. Nothing special needs to happen or be forced; I've found it has to do with the energy. It's so strange, just like the incident on a recent flight with a guy and girl sitting behind me. I was sleeping, minding my own business when I was suddenly awakened by two people fighting right behind me. I couldn't help but wonder, *Why was I getting drawn into this energy?*

Throughout these travels, trying to speak with the captain was never really on my radar. Maybe one day, I'd like to observe what goes on in the cockpit to broaden my scope of experiences in the air. However, the flight attendants are a different story – generally a very kind bunch, although some are not so nice! It's fascinating to see all the different personalities.

When flying, the focus is just to make it home. I thank God at take-off in gratitude that He has allowed me to be on the flight. I pray that the plane taxis safely down the runway and has a smooth take-off. Once in the air, it's time for meditation and total praise for Him to deliver us safely home. As the wheels touch down, "thank you again, Father!

CHAPTER 14

FRANCE/LYON

Scan QR code with phone
To See Chapter Preview

I think I am a good judge of people because I use my heart and not my head to reach a conclusion. The "Meeting" that took place on another long trip (from Grenoble, France, connecting through Lyon to London, heading back to the USA) was quite the surprise! My heart became fully engaged when I saw Ms. Lyon, France!

The flight was semi-crowded. I was resting well and had to use the bathroom. So, wiggling out of the chair, I headed down the aisle to the back of the plane. It's funny how your mind subconsciously scans the people sitting in the plane with you when you walk through those narrow aisles. Some people, for a second, stick to your eyes and mind, and others are like blurred figures. On this trip to the bathroom, though, my eye caught a fantastic energy that would touch a short season of my life, and I will never forget it.

Thanks to the "Meetings" at 35,000 Feet.

There she was, in the window seat about 7-8 rows from the aft bathroom on the plane. As I ambled down the aisle, I glanced over to where she was seated, and our eyes connected. At that exact moment, you could feel the heavy magnetic energy between us. There were no words, no physical contact, just beautiful communication space between us. As I glanced at her, she looked up again, and as our eyes held, she smiled slightly with an embarrassed look in her expression, somewhat shy. I smiled back with *it is okay* expression on my face and a heads-up nod.

The connection at that time seemed to pause, like the universe was telling me, *Yes, you need to know this person.* It's incredible to feel how your body reacts - how your heartbeat goes faster, a slight warmness comes to your body, and yes, your mind gets to wondering... *Who is she?* And her mind wonders... *Who is he? Why have we connected like this? Hmmm, this is very interesting.* It all goes through your mind in a flash. Some people call it animal instinct; I call it a universe connection from above.

As I strolled slowly past her row, I could see she still had a slight smile on her face. Stealing one more quick look, I glanced back at her again, but not too much; I didn't want her to think I was some pervert or weirdo!

I respect our women!

While I was in the bathroom, looking at the mirror and washing my face, my mind was saying, *keep it cool, Les;*

maybe that was just a moment in time, but both the universe and my heart were saying other things. Hearing this voice so often in my life has taught me to listen, act, and not dismiss it as a "coinkydink".

So, I took a deep breath, shrugged my shoulders, and puffed out my chest. Finally, I came and started to walk back towards my seat. As I neared her, I just wanted to know and to see if that same space connection of time would happen again!

Here I come to her row... She saw me out of the corner of her eye, and that same smile appeared, with a little more confidence of, *yes, I saw you.* And telepathically, I said, *yes I saw you, too,* in return. Once more, we shared that magical sense of mutual *wow* that required no words. It was a thrilling connection of just knowing, of agreement - and to have it happen at 35,000 feet, going 517 MPH was terrific!!!!

After that wow moment, I had no choice but to return back to my seat, and, of course, the juices started to flow. I wondered, *where is she from? Where is she going or coming from? What nationality is she?* ... She looked very exotic, with dark olive skin and black hair and large brown eyes. I have seen Ethiopian women look this way, but she looked more Arabic or Egyptian. My curiosity was getting the best of me. Of course, I couldn't go back down the aisle again to the bathroom, as the plane was going to land in 30 minutes, and she was sitting in the window seat. There was no way to talk to her, which would have just been too weird, obvious, and uncomfortable for everyone. She would have said for sure,

"What, does this guy have a bladder problem or something?" (lol).

So, I just sat there. Wondering. Full of curiosity and dismay.

Half an hour later, the plane landed, and everyone started to slowly disembark. In my mind, I was thinking, *I have to meet this person!*

Going into stealth mode from my aisle seat, I let the two people sitting next to me leave, so I could stay in my row, pretending I was gathering my stuff. *Hahahaha. Really.* That was me trying to buy time for her to reach my row so that we could finally meet with the same smile I saw earlier in the flight.

It was unbelievable!

I looked back in the plane where she was, and she saw exactly what I was doing, "playing the stalling game". She looked right at me and started to laugh and shake her head in amusement.

As she got closer and closer, we were eyeinng each other with anticipation as the people in front of her filed out one by one.

Finally, she reached my row, and there it was - a magnetic force field of attraction that drew us closer without words. A feeling I'd never felt before in my life, up until that moment on the plane. The first words of the "Meeting" that we said at the same time were, "Well, hello, how are you?" "Super," I said. "And you?" "Super, as well," she said. It was more smiles and slightly uncomfortable laughter, as we both said the same thing almost at the same time. Souls connecting with same thoughts. How funny that was. At this time, we knew there was a connection. The eye-to-eye contact was just so intense.

The next thing she did just blew my mind; she moved her body to the side row opposite mine to let the other passengers go by! It was like we knew each other, waiting to go out of the plane together as couples do. Well, we didn't know each other, but the universe knows better! I love a woman who knows who she is and is confident to show it when it is right and do it so classily and smoothly. I am sure everyone thought we knew each other, and she was simply waiting for her man to help her.

As we stood there in our row, in between a couple of the slower passengers coming out the aisle, I reached out my hand to her and said, "Nice to meet you". She extended her hand to me like a lady, and she said, "Nice to meet you, as well". There was that same smile I'd seen earlier while passing her row.

I am a good judge of character in first meetings. I could tell she was well taken care of by a hubby or an artist or fashion industry executive. She was dressed in all the latest fashion labels of the day, from MAC makeup to Jimmy Choo shoes, to the LV purse.

Not my kind of girl, but that smile and dark olive skin drew me to want to know more.

Right then and there, we did a rapid-fire of questions to see if we wanted to continue our "Meeting" or not. We were feeling each other out quickly.

What is your name?

Where are you coming from? Where are you going?

Are you alone or traveling to meet others?

To open the conversation, I said, "I saw you smiling at me." She said, "Yes," boldly, "and I saw you smiling at me, as well! So, I guess we both have beautiful smiles that attract positive people." That was like music to my ears; it was a clear signal that *I like you, and you like me, and there is no need to play the game to find out what is really happening here.*

As the last passengers left, we slowly walked the rest of the aisle, with her in front of me. We started asking point-blank questions to see how we could fit into each other's immediate travel agenda.

Are you in transit in London, or is London your final stop? I had a 4-hour layover before the next flight to Los Angeles; for her, London was her second home – she had a flat there she kept for business. As for her background, it turned out that she was Algerian/French, from Lyon. I was right on the money with my guess about her origins. I told her I was in Lyon for business in Grenoble. As we walked closer to the door, we decided to continue to talk to each other. I suggested she come to the American Airlines Executive Lounge to have a more extended conversation and get to know each other. You should have seen the flight attendants. They didn't want to push us off the plane during this "meeting", but at the same time, we were now the only two passengers left, literally standing in the aisle near the exit door. It was as if we didn't want the "meeting" on the plane to end, kind of like when you find yourself in a great dream about a sexy relationship - and you don't want to wake up to find it was just a dream.

It was set. The "Meeting" happened, the universe put the wheels in motion for the "Meaning" to be revealed, and now it was up to us.

We went out of the plane and continued to do the usual travel small talk. Still, I could tell she was nervous and anxious about *what this "Meeting" was and how it would evolve.*

We went to the American Airlines Executive lounge, got comfortable with drinks and appetizers, and the whole experience of the "Meeting", and the "Meaning" presented itself in full color.

Everything I had done in my life, she had done, from having children early, having grandchildren, being unhappily married, and just going through the motions to survive the relationship.

In the end, we had a relationship that lasted one year. It was a relationship of freedom, joy, peace, sadness, and transition. It was a relationship of soul mates that needed to be together to transfer them from one point of time to the next. The ocean or, as some say, the pond, was just too great for us to work… someone would have had to give up a lot. Neither of us was willing to give up grandchildren nearby, careers and family. But, at the same time, a love like that cannot do a long-distance relationship well. It was just too difficult.

It is incredible how "Meetings" at 35,000 feet can change you and move you to a new existence in time.

Thank you, Ms. Lyon, France; you taught me how to love again, unconditionally, to let go and remove the fear of that love.

CHAPTER 15

CAN'T WE ALL JUST GET ALONG?

I grew up at the time of the Crips and the Bloods in our neighborhood. I remember when our neighborhood was taken over by them; every time we came home from school, they were on the corner harassing and fighting with people.

We all had to defend ourselves.

I've seen my friends get killed by so-called wanna-be gangsters. I've seen people get maimed for no reason at all … except being in the wrong place at the wrong time… or wearing the wrong colors. In fact, my friend Tony got paralyzed by these gangsters. I was supposed to be in the car with him that day, but I had to be the responsible one as usual.

My friends and I wanted to have a party. So, we said, "Let's just get a hotel, invite everyone over, pay $50 to the security guard and be safe." We thought it would be a good idea because we didn't want to be out in the street with so much violence going on. I had a credit card, so I was the one who paid for the hotel room, and after I took care of that, I just waited there for the guys to come back with the goodies.

Tony and the other guys jumped in his car and went to get the drinks and all the other stuff we needed. But when they got back to the car after shopping, they got ambushed. A guy stuck his gun in the car before they could shut the door and said, "Give me all your stuff." Then Tony started fighting with the guy, and the gun went off. Tony got hit and, as a result, became paralyzed.

Violence can never be predicted; you never know where, when, or how; it will strike. Sometimes, it's just an eerie feeling that you get, and then it just happens. Fortunately, even as a teenager, I didn't get caught up in gang life or the drug scene. By the grace of God and my parent's teachings, I steered clear of that kind of trouble. Some kids aren't so fortunate to have good parenting, or they might live in a neighborhood infested with gangs and inescapable violence. Whenever I can, I try to talk some sense into these young bloods by volunteering as a "Big Brother".

You've got these naive kids in these neighborhoods, saying things like, *yo man, this is my block.* So, one day I said, "Oh really? When is the last time you went down to city hall, sat with the congressman or city commissioners, and really talked about how you could introduce programs to make things better in this block that you say is "yours"? Is your name on it, boy? If that's not the case, why are you talking about *this is your block?* And saying that you own this? You don't own anything; *they* make you live there because *they* want you to kill each other. So, wake up, you don't own anything. You're dying for the Bloods because they want you to. And you don't even see it... talking about *this is my block, this is my set.* Really?"

I've always had that mindset because of what my parents instilled in me. Both my parents come from 5th Ward Houston, which is not the prettiest place in the world. As a matter of fact, it's a pretty rough community. They had their struggles, but at the same time, my siblings and I were born in Los Angeles when all this stuff was happening, and we were constantly exposed to gangs and violence. In fact, my mom was around violence every day because she worked at the Charles Drew High School in South Los Angeles. She was teaching all these knuckleheads, these gangbangers, these kids who had no respect for authority. It wasn't necessarily their fault. They didn't have good parenting, they lived in a terrible environment, and they just didn't know any better.

My mom was in harm's way, all the time, every time she went to work. And as if she didn't have enough danger around her, one day, she chased after a couple of students who'd stolen a woman's purse. She was actually running down the street chasing them. When I found out what had happened, I said, "Mom, are you crazy? You always taught us to avoid trouble, and here you go chasing after those gangbangers!" She told me that she was so angry that she didn't even realize she was chasing them.

So, when I think about having gone through my teen years unscathed by all the dangers that could have crippled, killed, or imprisoned me, I think of how fortunate I am. But, I believe a lot of my good fortune comes from the fact that my parents instilled a positive attitude. I am a leader, not a follower, and that has made a big difference in how I tackled the world and always managed to build things rather than tear them down.

Now, as an executive vice president for an international company, I help with product design and development as well as global operations, sales, and marketing. Because of all these responsibilities, I avoid drama in my day-to-day life. I constantly talk to salespeople, product people, logistics people, just trying to get the product moved, or created, or sold.

God blessed me with the ability to see a need, envision a product that doesn't yet exist, and understand how it needs to be manufactured, marketed, and distributed. My job is to function as the brain at the center and keep my team pulling in the same direction.

All total, we have approximately 20-25 people working globally, including about 15 salespeople. Most of the action is in China, where we have about 500 people working in the factory. So, I am around people all the time – employees, business associates, customers, and prospects; and I am definitely a frequent flier who spends 75% of his life in the air. Whether working in my office or traveling to a regional or international meeting, I tend to remain calm, avoiding people or situations that could erupt into violence of any kind. Yet, you can never predict when it will find you. And you certainly would not expect it to be sitting practically in your lap on a flight, traveling across the country.

CHAPTER 16

DOMESTIC VIOLENCE ON A FLIGHT...
NOT TOLERATED

Another *crazy* story happened on my flight from Miami to LAX…

Flying at 35,000 feet and witnessing a "Meeting" of two people having a physical domestic violent argument is just not cool at all. There is no "Meaning" that I can think that justifies two people hitting and screaming at each other in an airplane these days. The FAA regulations and the power that airlines have these days are great. Level 1-4 codes of violence are well-documented, and procedures are in place to handle these situations. There are still Air Marshals on the planes, just waiting to take control.

I was flying back from Miami to LAX on a late-night flight. All was well, and I got an upgrade to 2C. Behind me was a young couple in 3C and 3B. They were having fun with each other, enjoying the boarding of the flight, and I could tell they had been drinking. But still, they were laughing, enjoying each other, and talking about their little vacation trip in Miami.

Halfway through the flight, while I was sleeping, I felt a hard, seemingly deliberate punch on the back of my chair. I could hear them starting to have a huge argument and hitting each other. Apparently, when the girl was asleep, the guy was going through her phone, found out that she had been text-messaging some other guys, and just lost it. He started screaming at her in the middle of the flight, saying, "Who are these people? Why are you text messaging them while you are with me? I brought you on this trip, and this is how you are going to do me?"

The girl was in full defense mode, saying, "You shouldn't have been going through my phone while I was asleep!" ...and back and forth, back and forth they went. Suddenly, they started yelling louder, cursing, and then they started hitting each other again.

Everyone in first class, including myself, turned around to see what the hell was going on. The flight attendants acted quickly and ran over to calm the situation. One of the flight attendants said, "Hey, stop it, both of you. You guys cannot be having domestic violence and yelling at each other while in flight." The couple said, "Mind your own business, lady". But the flight attendant said, "No, this is not tolerated, and I and others in first-class witnessed you hitting each other and yelling. This is a level 2 offense, and I am reporting it to the captain. If you continue, I will call the air marshals that are on this flight to restrain you by handcuff!"

The flight attendant called the captain by phone, and the decision was made that one of them had to move seats for the rest of the 2-hour flight. The couple went back and forth about why it happened and didn't want to separate, but the flight attendant and captain now had the power.

She said, "You have one more time to comply with my request, or we will restrain both of you for the rest of the flight, and charges will be brought against you when we land."

The couple discussed the situation, and the guy decided he would go to 9C for the rest of the flight. The girl remained in 3B and went to sleep.

The rest of the flight, thank God, was quiet. When we landed, the police immediately came on the flight, escorted them off the plane, and took them away for questioning.

Once again, even at this "Meeting" at 35,000 feet, it shows there's a "Meaning" to having physical domestic or verbal violence. It just won't be tolerated, and reinforces that people need to control their situation and emotions at all times, not just in flight.

CHAPTER 17

TURBULENCE...WEATHER ...OR NOT

Air Turbulence is a term for an instability in the air around a plane caused by winds, air pressure, temperature differentials, nearby storms, jet streams, weather fronts, and other atmospheric conditions. In aviation, turbulence is categorized by severity, from light to extreme.

Turbulence is certainty a significant source of flight anxiety for flyers of all stripes. Understanding what causes turbulence, where it occurs, and the high-tech tools pilots use to make air travel safer and more comfortable, may help settle even the most anxious flyer's nerves.

Rough air happens everywhere, from ground level to far above cruising altitude. But the most common turbulence experienced by flyers has three common causes: mountains, jet streams, and storms. Just as ocean waves break on a beach, air also forms waves as it encounters mountains. While some air passes smoothly over and onward, some air masses crowd against the mountains themselves, left with nowhere to go but up. These "mountain waves" can propagate as wide, gentle oscillations into the atmosphere, but they can also break up into many tumultuous currents, which we experience as turbulence.

Even for seasoned jet setters, turbulence can be an unnerving experience. Turbulence in an aircraft is like hitting a pothole in your car. Instead of a crumbling tarmac, the plane is coming into contact with chaotic eddies of air. These are swirling patterns of disrupted airflow that can be produced in a number of ways, such as cold and warm air meeting, jet streams, storms, or simply flying over mountains. Hitting these "waves" of airflow causes sudden changes to the plane's altitude or tilt, which results in the plane rocking around. In most instances, the aircraft likely isn't actually dipping and dodging as much as your gut might tell you.

Certain conditions can make planes more likely to experience a nasty bout of turbulence, such as the presence of mountain ranges and stormy cumulonimbus clouds. (Cumulonimbus clouds are dense, vertical, towering clouds commonly associated with instability in the atmosphere and thunderstorms. The cumulonimbus cloud is formed by water vapor that air currents carry upwards. These clouds can produce dangerous lightning and severe tornadoes.)

Although turbulence is often unavoidable, pilots can usually work out where the rough areas will be located by looking at weather forecasts and wind variability data. In fact, most modern aircraft use algorithms to keep tabs on high turbulence zones. Vertical currents caused by thunderstorms are arguably the most problematic of the bunch, although they are relatively easy for pilots to spot and avoid.

Turbulence is the bane of every nervous flyer, from those with a mild fear of flying to those who carry their own barf bags when they travel. Here are five things you need to know the next time the pilot asks you to buckle up for a bumpy ride:

1. It's Not as Scary as It Seems...

Though it ranks as perhaps the #1 concern of airline passengers, turbulence during a flight is perfectly normal and rarely puts the aircraft in jeopardy. In really rare cases, it can injure people and damage aircraft. Still, in practice, it's a comfort and convenience issue rather than a safety issue. *In the passengers' minds, the plane is plummeting hundreds or thousands of feet, but pilots might only see a twitch of 10 or 20 feet on the altimeter.*

2. No, Your Plane Isn't Going Down

Consider that in the history of aviation, turbulence has been the culprit in only a handful of crashes. Most notably, on 1966 British Overseas Airways Flight 911 from Tokyo to Hong Kong, a pilot changed routing so the passengers could get a closer look at Mt. Fuji - only to be overwhelmed by extremely violent air currents (possibly exacerbated by the mountain) that took off the tail fin of the Boeing 707 and caused it to fall to the ground. Although it's unlikely that modern aircraft would suffer the same problems, all 124 people aboard were killed.

Still, turbulence can be a serious matter, causing injury or even death, even if it doesn't bring an entire modern plane down. The vast majority of these incidents happen when passengers aren't buckled in their seats. Because of the nature of their responsibilities, crew members are far more likely to be hurt during turbulence than actual passengers.

Clear air turbulence, or "CAT", is the least predictable or observable type of disturbance. CAT is often the culprit behind moderate to severe injuries, as it can occur so suddenly that flight crew members don't have time to instruct passengers to buckle up. According to the Federal Aviation Administration, *524 passengers and crew were reported injured by turbulence between 2002 and 2017.*

3. Turbulence Is Not Always Avoidable

You should resign yourself to experiencing *some* turbulence on just about any flight. Where you are in the world or what time of day or night doesn't guarantee or offer a respite from turbulence. Rest assured that, in the cockpit, the crew is doing everything they can do to avoid or minimize it.

Modern technology is a wonder, with airline meteorologists providing up-to-the-minute weather models to steer planes away from the worst areas. Pilots also help each other out with updates. When turbulence is unavoidable, pilots may also slow down their aircraft to keep the shake to a minimum. Each particular aircraft model has what's known as its turbulence penetration speed, which is its ideal velocity for getting through rough air.

4. It's Worse in the Back of the Plane

Though bigger planes like A380s and 747s tend to absorb turbulence better than smaller ones, there aren't any hard and fast rules about which aircraft are better at handling it than others. If you feel like you're getting a rougher ride in Row 40 than your friends in first class, you're probably right. The smoothest seats tend to be in the center of the plane over the wing because that's closest to the plane's center of lift and gravity.

5. Buckle Your Seatbelt.

By now, you should realize that the seatbelt sign doesn't go on during a flight just because the pilots are maliciously trying to keep you from using the bathroom. The single best thing you can do when turbulence hits is to get into your seat and buckle up.

Everyone has a story about hitting a rough patch of air, those hair-raising moments when suddenly more than the plane is flying. Bellies drop, drinks slop, and people caught in the aisle lurch against seats. In rare cases, it can even mean more than bumps or bruises. I am a seasoned veteran with over 3,000,000 miles under my belt, and I will *never* be comfortable with turbulence…

CHAPTER 18

MIAMI CROSS WINDS... DON'T MESS WITH MOTHER NATURE

Ok, in this "Meeting" at 35,000 feet, I learned that Mother Nature is in control, despite some believing they can command her, based on their technology and their big a** Egos.

I was taking a flight from LAX to Miami during the hurricane season. I took that flight on the tail end of a hurricane, thinking that the majority of the winds and rains would be gone and everything coming into Miami would be smooth.

Wrong.

The flight into Miami that day was everything but smooth. It was choppy all the way from Texas to Miami. It was clear that the weather pattern was still picking up storm activities, and we were right in the middle of it.

The plane was going up and down like a yo-yo. The pilot tried everything to find smooth air! He went up, then down, then he went left, and then right. He finally came on the intercom and apologized that he couldn't find smooth air and that we would have a rough ride the rest of the way into Miami.

You know it is an issue when they cancel the second beverage service and tell the flight attendants to be seated for the duration of the flight. He was right to do so. We were hitting air pockets that would drop the plane 500 feet at a time!

Some people screamed when this happened, and some people thought it was fun. Especially the young adults. Others put their hands in the air, just like they were on an air-free roller coaster ride!

Unfortunately for me, I was worried because a little girl (maybe 10 years old) was sitting next to me in the middle. I was in the aisle seat. She was traveling alone from LA to meet her family on the other side of the country, in Miami. Before the flight attendants had to sit down, they checked on her and could tell she was nervous. I told the flight attendant I would look after her, and they thanked me. Maria was her name, and this was her second time flying in her life. She said the first flight to LA was smooth, and she said she was scared of the way the plane was moving. I told her, no worries, everything would be ok and just think of it as a ride at a carnival. *Such bulls**t*, this thing was moving up and down like riding a mechanical bull in a country bar!

Porbresita

I felt for Maria because there was no escaping it. The lady next to her in the window seat tried to calm her as well, with her motherly instincts and companionship. It seemed to help a little.

Now, what happened next was just ridiculous.

The pilot came on the horn and tried to explain that the "crosswinds" into the Miami airport were 60-70 knots, that it would be a rocky landing, and to relax because they do this all the time. I thought to myself, *ok, we need to go land in another airport. This is not a time to show your pilot skills or to have a macho air show landing with us!*

He further explained that the plane would be rocking left to right and vice versa on the runway approach. I thought to myself, again, *this guy has got to be kidding me. Is he crazy?*

Then, the pilot said, "Flight attendants, make sure everyone is fastened in, and all things are put away." You should have seen the flight attendants trying to go up and down the aisle to check on people. They were grabbing the backs of the chairs to brace themselves while they were walking. It was just out of this world. You could hear the winds against the walls of the plane- that's how bad they were blowing.

I have been on many flights from the USA to Hong Kong, and you would swear there was an evil wind monster on the outside of the plane, ready to pull the plane down to earth. *Those of you who've been through that flight to Asia know what I am talking about.* Sometimes the plane can drop 1,000 feet on those flights; you feel like your stomach is in your mouth. The only thing you can do is say a prayer, tighten your belt, and breathe. Some people just put a blanket over their heads and sleep through it because there is nothing you can do to escape it. The turbulence can last up to 2 hours, which I also have experienced.

Back to this crazy Miami flight. Once we started our approach, the pilot came back on the horn and again stated his plan to take us through these cross winds and how he would ensure everything would be alright. At this point, I knew it was his Ego that made him even consider taking on Mother Nature and that we would be the victims of it.

As we approached the airport, you could feel the winds getting stronger. Sure enough, just as the pilot had said, the plane was tilting back and forth, left to right. He couldn't hold it level - it was swaying 45-50 degrees!

You could tell he was having difficulty leveling off for the approach; when he tried to correct the plane, there was a jerking motion back the other way. At this point, people were panicking – even the thrill-seekers. Maria was in pure fright and in tears. She said she was scared and asked us to hold her hands. The lady and I grabbed María's hands, and we held her very tightly. She was crying hard now.

People in the plane were no longer raising their hands. Instead, they were grabbing onto the armrests and screaming every time the pilot overcorrected. I even heard the flight attendants near us, say, "This is damn crazy."

I couldn't believe that this guy was going to try to land this plane in these crosswinds. I have flown thousands of times in my life, and I could tell this was a thrill-seeking venture for this guy!

So, as we started to approach the runway, the plane was still tilting back and forth; I know from experience that *there was no way to land this thing when it was rocking so violently.* The winds had us; they were saying, "Ahh, you want to challenge us, then I will show you!" We were approximately 500 feet from the runway, and the wind blew so hard that it flipped the plane's tilt about 65 degrees. The pilot tried to compensate back in the other direction... and everyone on the plane just lost it. We were all screaming, "Pull up, pull up!", even the flight attendants. But just before he would have had to touch down, the pilot put the engines into full acceleration and PULLED up drastically!!!! *I freakin' couldn't believe that this guy was going to try that damn landing!!!*

Poor María was hysterical and, poor baby, she peed in her pants. I think she had to go to the bathroom but was so frightened to move that she just peed right there in the chair.

I was hot as "white coals" on a BBQ pit. As we elevated up quickly, everyone was incensed and yelling about what our pilot had just tried to do. WTF!

He came on the intercom again and tried to apologize for the approach. You should have heard all the things people were saying to him. I am sure, through his locked cockpit door, he could hear the curses from the passengers:

You a**hole! I thought.

MF!

You could have killed us! You crazy SOB!

What the hell is wrong with you! Etc. etc.

The flight attendants tried to calm people, but they were not having it. They felt that the pilot had tried a daredevil move and that it was uncalled for. He could have crashed the plane on that runway.

He explained that the crosswinds were too much for the landing, and this is why he pulled up.

No shit, Sherlock! People were saying, "No shit, MF! You could have killed us. You are crazy for even trying!"

He explained that they called the tower to ask for a runway that was facing the headwinds so that the landing approach would be more straightforward and there would be very few crosswinds.

Everyone was yelling. "Why didn't you do that the first time!?"

As I said at the beginning of this story, Mother Nature is in control despite man and his big a** Ego thinking he can control her.

When you hear from the pilot to buckle your seat belts and that the landing approach will be rocky, you will think of this story and either laugh or get worried. Try to laugh and hope your pilot is not like this crazy a**hole we had!

Finally, we the landing again. The pilot swings the plane around to approach for a headwind landing. It was much smoother in tilt, but now we really heard the wind and felt the plane's drag on the front. We got closer and closer to the runway. I was holding Maria's hand, and she was closing her eyes tight.

We went lower and lower, and *boom!* We landed. The plane was swerving left and right, and the pilot was doing his best to keep it straight. You could hear the rubber tires gripping the ground and making scratching noises as he pumped the brakes slowly to not go into a full skid mode. Finally, he got the damn plane in control, and it came to a complete stop.

Everyone was relieved, and all of a sudden started to scream with joy. They were hugging each other, clapping, thanking God, etc. Poor María was a mess. She had tears in her eyes, pee in her pants, and her hair was everywhere. I think this child will never take a plane ride again and will have trauma for life.

The pilot came on the intercom one last time. Everyone started screaming at him, calling him every name in the book. He parked the plane, and everyone started to file out. They wanted to know what the pilot's name was, so they could file a complaint or a lawsuit. People were pissed. As we deplaned, the pilot didn't open the cockpit door, as is customary. He knew if he opened that door, the passengers would have dragged him into the airport concourse by his a**. As people passed by, almost everyone slammed their hand on the door or banged their fists on it, saying, "You coward, you a**hole, I am going to sue you! You could have killed us!"

The flight attendants came for María; she looked at us with tears in her eyes and said, "Thank you so much." We said, "It is going to be ok, María." She started crying again as they took her off the plane, wet and still terrified.

As we got off the plane, I heard people calling the police, asking for the airport manager and just waiting for the pilot to come out of the plane. He never came out. The authorities did come, and they took people's statements of what happened. I wondered to myself if this would come out in the press. To this day, I'm still not sure, and   I never heard of a lawsuit or news report.

The "Meaning" of this flight at 35,000 feet is that the pilot who tried to test Mother Nature was an idiot ruled by his Ego, and Mother Nature, once again, showed us who is boss.

Don't try to take on things that could damage other people's lives, including your own. Always think of safety first versus pushing the odds. If you are going to do it, do it on your own time and risk your own life. You have free will…but no sovereignty over others. Good luck with that Ego and your Karma. Don't make your journey someone else's journey and Karma path.

Sorry, Mother Nature, again, you showed your strength, and we just need to honor you. Love and peace.

CHAPTER 19

WHAT'S IN A HANDSHAKE?

Check this out. This is deep! PRE-Covid-19

Warriors in the Indian, African, Greek, and Roman days were protective of their tribes. They cautiously approached strangers with spear or knife in hand to make it very clear they were armed. The stranger would have to use some type of verbal "calling" well in advance to let the warriors know that he came in peace and not as an enemy.

A handshake is perhaps one of the oldest forms of introductory communication, dating back thousands of years. Though its origins are murky, a popular theory is that it began to relay peaceful intentions. A person would extend their empty right hand to show a stranger they were not   holding weapons and did not have ill will toward them.

This approach lasted for many years until things started to get more civilized and the actual handshake was created. A handshake is the same as the "calling". When you reach out to shake someone's hand, it means, "I come in peace." It means I am not your enemy. The up-and-down motion is thought to have been a means of removing any knives or daggers hidden up a sleeve. I am sure you have felt different types of handshakes. Through those handshakes, even without words, you can tell a lot about the person, their intentions, and what he or she wants to convey to you.

Can you imagine today using callings or walking into a meeting with a spear and knife in hand? *There's a pretty funny picture.*

A handshake is also thought to have been a symbol of good faith when making an oath or promise. Today, handshakes serve as a form of introduction meant to initiate conversation, whether in a social setting or a professional one. But it holds a lot more weight than just serving as an unspoken greeting. Handshakes reveal a lot about the type of person you are and how you feel in the situation. Find out if your handshake is working for or against you and how you can ensure you do it right every time.

A **handshake** is a globally widespread, brief greeting or parting tradition in which two people grasp one of each other's like hands. In most cases, it's accompanied by a brief up-and-down movement. Handshakes are sometimes used to signify romantic relationships.

Using the right hand is generally considered proper etiquette, but the customs surrounding handshakes are culture-specific. Different cultures may be more or less likely to shake hands, or there may be additional customs about how and when to shake hands.

From too firm, too limp, too rushed, or too long, people judge a lot about you by your handshake. I have to chuckle whenever I think of President Trump's handshake with French President Emmanuel Macron. It seems that U.S. President Donald Trump met his match in a handshake showdown with the French president. At their first meeting, ahead of a NATO summit in Brussels, the two men locked hands for so long that knuckles started turning white. Trump finally seemed ready to pull away -- but Macron evidently wasn't. The French leader held the shake for a few seconds more. Both men's jaws seemed to clench. (*It wasn't exactly what is referred to as a Politician's Handshake.*)

HERE ARE SOME EXAMPLES OF HANDSHAKE STYLES:

1) THE DOMINANT HANDSHAKE

Research shows that handshakes matter, and some think that a dominant handshake goes in too hard. You never want the other person to feel like you're trying to take the upper hand by forcing their palm up. Lillian Glass, Ph.D., a renowned body language expert based in Beverly Hills, California, says, "Shaking someone's hand too hard shows competition. It's a power struggle."

2) THE LIMP HANDSHAKE

When you go in for a handshake with someone, and it feels like their hand is nonexistent, how does it make you feel?

According to Dr. Glass, "A weak handshake exemplifies a lack of interest. If you lack all firmness, it tells the other person you don't care; you're not into them." Whether it's a stranger or a professional, people are sensitive toward your gestures. They will likely form immediate judgments from your handshake that set the tone of your circumstances.

3) THE POLITICIAN'S HANDSHAKE

When the initiator places both hands on the other person's, this is a sign of honesty and trust. "It's not a power trip; it's a liking trip," Dr. Glass says. "And when the initiator uses their free hand to grasp the receiver's elbow, it says, 'I really, really like you.'"

4) THE RUSHED HANDSHAKE

Rushing a handshake as quickly as you come out shows nervousness. According to Dr. Glass, "People who can't hold on for a moment to establish the introduction show discomfort. It also shows that they really don't care to be in the situation at all, which offends the receiver." Rushing anything typically never makes for a positive outcome, so slow it down to generate calmness.

5) THE LOOK AWAY HANDSHAKE

A lack of eye contact is more than just awkward. It's rude. "If you make immediate eye contact but then look away, you're showing disinterest and awkwardness," says Dr. Glass. Handshakes are supposed to help ease any introductory tension, not add to it. This type of handshake is often associated with a rushed one.

6) THE LINGERING HANDSHAKE

Going in with a good firm grasp that's not knuckle-grinding is important, but when you don't let go, it gives off desperation. Though you definitely don't want to rush it, try not to hold on for longer than two full seconds.

7) THE INTENSE GLARE HANDSHAKE

"If you stare into someone's eyes for too long as your handshake lingers, you're showing aggression," according to Dr. Glass. "Don't purse your lips and squint your eyes," she advises.

8) THE PERFECT HANDSHAKE

A handshake can mean many different things. According to Dr. Glass, "A good handshake entails the initiator's palm touching the receiver's palm, with their thumb wrapped around the other's thumb. Connecting through touch sends the message of friend instead of foe." You want to make sure your grasp is firm, but not too firm, and definitely not too light. "Always maintain eye contact, but ensure you have a soft, warm gaze. Any intense glare is to be   avoided."

Pre-Covid-19, it felt very awkward when others would not shake   your hand. It was the weirdest feeling in the world to extend your hand, and the other person left you hanging… especially if you hadn't met previously.

In those days, such a failure made you ask *what the f**k is wrong with this person?* Your alarm bells would start going off right then and there, and you'd wish you had your ancient spear or knife in hand to let this person know you are on guard! That gesture truly meant this person didn't want to have anything to do with you, they were an introvert or a germophobe.

Now with Covid-19, everything has changed. Now we have the new "Elbow Shake".

As I have noted above, Pre-Covid-19, the handshake was commonly done upon meeting, greeting, parting, offering congratulations, expressing gratitude, or as a public sign of completing a business or diplomatic agreement. In sports or other competitive activities, it is also a sign of good sportsmanship. Its purpose is to convey trust, respect, balance, and equality. If it is done to seal an agreement, the agreement is not official until the hands are parted.

Unless health issues or local customs dictate otherwise, a handshake is usually made with bare hands. However, it depends on the situation.

There are various customs surrounding handshakes, both generically and specific to certain cultures. For instance:

- In Anglophone countries, handshaking is common in business situations. In casual non-business cases, men are more likely to shake hands than women.

- In the Netherlands and Belgium, handshakes are done more often, especially in meetings.

- In Switzerland, it may be expected to shake the women's hands first.

- Austrians shake hands when meeting, often including meeting with children, as well.

- In the United States, a traditional handshake is firm, executed with the right hand, with good posture & eye contact.

- In Russia, a handshake is performed by men and rarely performed by women.

- In some countries, such as Turkey or the Arabic-speaking Middle East, handshakes are not as firm as in the West. Consequently, a grip that is too firm is rude. Hand-shaking between men and women is not encouraged in the Arabic world. Also, only the right hand should be used.

- Moroccans also give one kiss on each cheek (to corresponding genders) together with the handshake. Also, in some countries, a variation exists where, instead of kisses and the handshake, the palm is placed on the heart.

- In China, a weak handshake is also preferred. Still, people shaking hands often hold on to each other's hands for an extended period, after the initial handshake.

- In Japan, it is appropriate to let the Japanese initiate the handshake, and a weak handshake is preferred. The Japanese do not have a tradition of shaking hands, preferring to formally bow with hands open by their sides, but will greet non-Japanese with a handshake.

- In India and several nearby countries, the respectful Namaste gesture, sometimes combined with a slight bow, is traditionally used in place of handshakes. However, handshakes are preferred in business and other formal settings.

- In Norway, where a firm handshake is preferred, people will most often shake hands when agreeing on private and business relations deals.

- In Korea, a senior person will initiate a handshake, which is preferred to be weak. It is a sign of respect to grasp the right arm with the left hand when shaking hands. It is disrespectful to have your free hand in your pocket while shaking hands. It is also considered disrespectful to put one's hand in your pocket while shaking another person's hand. Bowing is the preferred and conventional way of greeting a person in Korea.

- Related to a handshake but more casual, some people prefer a fist bump. Typically, the fist bump is done with a clenched hand; only the knuckles touch the knuckles of the other person's hand. Like a handshake, the fist bump may be used to acknowledge a relationship with another person. However, unlike a handshake's formality, the fist bump is typically not used to seal a business deal or in formal business settings.

- The hand hug is a type of handshake popular with politicians. It can present them as being warm, friendly, trustworthy, and honest. This type of handshake involves covering the clenched hands with the remaining free hand, creating a sort of "cocoon".

- Another version popular with politicians is a "photo-op handshake" in which, after the initial grasp, both individuals turn to face photographers and cameramen and stay this way for several seconds.

- As a gesture of trust, Scouts will shake hands with their left hand, which originated when founder Lord Baden-Powell of Gillwell, then a British cavalry officer, met an African tribesman.

- In some areas of Africa, handshakes are continually held to show that the conversation is between the two talking. If they are not shaking hands, others are permitted to enter the conversation.

- Masai men in Africa greet one another with a brief, subtle touch of the palms of their hands.

- In Liberia, the snap handshake is customary, in which the two shakers snap their fingers against each other after the handshake.

CHAPTER 20

PARTNER IN THE SKY

I, one hundred percent, without a doubt, believe that God, the Universe, and man/woman within this cosmic realm are connected as one. With no judgment or Ego, it is apparent that all you have to do is wake up and see with the heart, spirit, and mind how these connections work. If you are really tapped in, you can see how they work on your behalf and how you can flow within them and allow the circumstance(s) to work through you for good. Even when you experience trials and tribulations, just flow with them because they shall pass, and you will see why you had to go through them.

We all go through Trials and Tribulations, but they only last a little while. Smooth waters always await.

Most people fear the trials and tribulations, run from them, or try to force them to go away. Instead, suppose you embrace them, seek understanding, and are open to ask without fear why and how you can learn something from the experience when it passes. In that case, you will see why you were brought into it and why you needed to go through it.

Sometimes it is simply to teach you a lesson and make you stronger. Sometimes, it moves you in a new direction; when one door closes, another one opens. You look back and go *ahhh... that is why that happened.* Please don't say that it is good luck, bad luck, or a quinkidink... it is the universe. God and his angels were working on your behalf.

In the Good and Bad times, God states, you will have trials and tribulations on this earth. It is how you handle these situations that gives you character and wisdom.

For example, when a family member is going to pass away, a baby is often born into the family. It is almost as if God knows he will transition this spirit from the body that we are used to seeing, talking to, and feeling. And then we experience the trials and tribulations of sorrow and pain once they are gone. A baby, a child, or even a puppy comes into the family at that time of transition. That new life in the family provides a bridge of happiness and remembrance of the true love and compassion to the person they left.

I say this because nothing happens in our lives for *just because*. People come in and out of our lives for "meanings".

Here is an example of a partner I met in the sky at "35,000" feet and the "Meaning" behind that "Meeting".

I was catching a flight from Panama to LAX during the summertime. As the universe usually does to make sure I rest well, it provided me an upgrade on the flight. *Thank you, universe.* I place the intention, and if the universe grants it, then so be it. If not, I really look forward to seeing who I am going to sit next to!

I had an aisle seat, and the window seat next to me was empty. As usual, people were piling into the plane, one by one.

I noticed a family of three coming onto the plane, laughing, enjoying each other, and in good spirits. It is always refreshing to see a happy family having a good time on a trip together.

The next thing I knew, the family stopped by my aisle. The wife sat in front of me, the son behind me, and the husband in the empty window seat. It was almost like a dotted connection of souls joined together in a "triangle".

The husband sat down, got settled in, and looked over at me. With a beautiful smile, he said, "Hello, I am WR." I said hello back; "I am Les Dotson," and we shook hands. I didn't know then what I know today about handshakes and how powerful they are.

The handshake between WR and me was firm, solid, and confident. It was a *perfect* handshake that was also met with eye-to-eye contact saying, *hey, I am not your enemy, and honestly welcome your spirit to mine.*

WR went one step further; he introduced me to his wife sitting in front of me. She was just as friendly and inviting with a handshake, and then WR introduced me to his son, and we shook hands. It was clear this family was bonded with the same energy flow, love, and togetherness. They were in sync, with the same high vibration, which I have come to learn over these years, truly exists. And people can resonate with this energy by using these simple body language gestures.

WR and I started to talk about ourselves. He explained that they were coming from Costa Rica to pick up his son from a retreat. I shared with him that I was doing business in Panama for HP/Dell and was on my way home to Los Angeles to see my family.

Now the "Meeting" began between WR and me, and the "Meanings" would change our life paths for the rest of our lives!

After WR introduced his family to me, we began the usual small chat. He explained that he and the family would catch a connecting flight from Costa Rica to Panama to LAX. They were having a family vacation for the summer. I told WR that I was in Panama working with Dell and HP and setting up some productions for Colombia and Peru to diversify the supply chain.

He said, "Really? I also did some marketing work for HP." Turns out WR was a marketing guru who'd been in the marketing, web, and entertainment side of the business and had worked with celebrities and music entertainers. WR stated that he'd done a marketing piece for *Beats by Dre* co-branded with HP. I said, "I also did a Marketing piece and product for *Beats by Dre* for HP." *It was the same marketing campaign!* – for the HP *Beats by Dre* laptop with the *Beats by Dre* sleeve, which covered and protected the laptop. It was a massive marketing campaign, and many marketing companies and product companies were involved.

We both were amazed that we were sitting next to each other and had worked on the same project. *How the universe works on our behalf!*

After this strong connection of product, marketing, advertising, design, and manufacturing, we had quite the synergy between each other.

We talked for 5 hours straight on the plane about every aspect of the businesses we were in over 20+ years. Despite totally different family backgrounds and cultures, it was like meeting my "brother from another mother". The "meaning" of the connection was music - WR played drums in a rock band, and I played professional trumpet - the arts, entertainment, and sports markets. Up to this moment, I was primarily into the B2B and Consumer Electronics markets with product development.

I was always fascinated how *Beats by Dre,* which was purchased by Apple for $3.2 billion, went from street hip-hop music to headphones for sports, millennials, and ultimately to corporate America. How many times did I see first-class passengers who had worn nothing but boring Bose headphones for years, now wearing *Beats By Dre* headphones? The brand captured these markets less than 5 years after launch and took over 70 percent market share.

Amazing!

By the time we hit the tarmac in Los Angeles, WR and I both knew we had to work together on a project. That thought became a reality. We created a bond of friendship and business partnership that has run deep for 8 years now. We have experienced every aspect of business and met tons of brilliant people in all industries. Our friendship has grown and flourished, and we have created a network of just high vibration people around us. It is like a family community.

Such unique synergy - staying out of each other's lane professionally, but at the same time, building a brotherhood to last a lifetime. This is the "Meaning" of this "Meeting" at 35,000 feet... partner in the sky.

Love and peace to my "brother from another mother".

CHAPTER 21

MAKING THE MOST
OF YOUR FREE TIME

If you have a big block of free time, the best way to put that to use is to relax, have fun, decompress from a stressful day, or spend time talking with a loved one or a new acquaintance. But if you've just got a little chunk — say 5, 10, 15, or 20 minutes — there's probably no time to do any of the fun stuff...but maybe you can spruce up your bank account...

You've just boarded your cross-country flight, and you've got 20 minutes before takeoff. Most of us might just sit down, settle in, read, or people watch. But some of us might use our time a bit more productively. For instance, why not make a little pocket change before losing the signal on your cell phone? Before you decide, here are some things to consider putting those little chunks of time towards, to be the most productive during your travels.

Everyone works differently, so the best use of your free time really depends on you, your working style, and what's on your "to-do list". It's handy to have a list like this to quickly find a way to put that spare time to work almost instantly, ...or better yet, with precise, and well-organized planning.

1. Set Up a Reading File

Before you travel, clip magazine articles or print out good articles or reports for reading on your trip, and keep them in a folder marked "Reading File". Take this wherever you go, and any time you have a little chunk of time, you can knock off items in your Reading File. Or, while you are on the plane, set up a file on your laptop for quick reading.

2. Clear out Your Inbox

Got a few minutes? Use it to check emails and or empty your inbox. You may not get everything done, but reducing your pile can be a big help, and having an empty inbox is a wonderful feeling.

3. Make Phone Calls

Keep a list of phone calls you need to make, with phone numbers, and carry it everywhere. Before takeoff, you can knock a few calls off your list in a short amount of time.

4. Network

Only have 2 minutes? Shoot off a quick email to a colleague. Even just a "touching bases" or follow-up email can do wonders for your working relationship. Or shoot off a quick question and put it on your follow-up list for later.

5. Plan Your Goals

Take 10 minutes to think about your goals — personal and professional. If you don't have a list of goals, start on one. If you've got a list of goals, review them. Write down a list of action steps you can take over the next couple of weeks to make these goals a reality. What action step can you do today? The more you focus on these goals and review them, the more likely they will come true.

6. Brainstorm Ideas

If you just have 5 minutes — break out your pocket notebook and start a brainstorming list for a project. Whatever you've got coming up in your work or personal life can benefit from a brainstorming session. And that doesn't take long.

7. Follow up

Keep a follow-up list for everything you're waiting on. Return calls, emails, memos — anything that someone owes you, put on the list. When you've got a spare 10 minutes, do some follow-up calls or emails.

8. Meditate or Pray

You don't need a yoga mat to do this; your seat will do just fine. Focus on your breathing. A quick 5 to 10 minutes of meditation or prayer can be tremendously refreshing. Shut out all the sounds and all the people around you (this works best in a window seat).

9. Get Prepped

Outlining is one way to prep for more extended work, but there are many other ways you can prep for the next task on your list. You may not have time to actually start on the job right now,   but when you arrive at your destination or come back from your trip, you'll be all prepped and ready to go.

10. Make Money

This is my favorite productive use of free time. Usually, when I am flying, I am on my way to or from a business meeting. As executive vice president for Swiss luggage and backpack company, Swissdigital Backpacks, I focus on product design and development, global operations, sales, and marketing daily. And all those conversations spent talking to salespeople, product people, and logistics people get the product moved, created, or sold. You could say that I am the brain at the center of it all.

These products were my creation – I'm blessed with the ability to see something and bring it to life. *I was able to see the product in my mind, understand the issues and how they needed to be solved, design a good-looking and functional product, and manufacture it.* We have about 20-25 people working globally; most of the action is in China. We have about 15 salespeople and about 500 in the factory.

So, I have a list of calls to select from, whether to generate income, start new projects, or beef up production. Usually, when awaiting takeoff, I am either gathering my thoughts, planning a meeting, making a last-minute call, or texting final instructions to someone. But in reality, I am making money during the 20-30 minute boarding process. During my "free time" on one of my recent cross-country flights, however, I was one-upped by a Swiss watch broker who was also *Making Money*…lots of money…

CHAPTER 22

HIGH-END SWISS WATCH DEAL
"MEETING" GOING DOWN AT 35,000 FEET
WHAT A "MEANING"!!!!

Made in Switzerland

My friends; some of us bro's have a craving for high-end Swiss watches, just like our ladies may have a passion for high-end shoes and purses. It's all good to like these material things in life. They are made for us to admire, aspire to, or show a certain status. When it comes to high-end Swiss watches, some love them purely for the beauty of their craftsmanship, as each one is handmade in Switzerland. Every part is well-engineered and placed, piece by piece, to keep track of the "time" we chase every day of our lives. So when we look down on our wrists at that piece of steel with its custom band, we think, *Damn, that is a beautiful piece of machinery.* This Swiss know-how is unrivaled.

The excellence of Swiss craftsmanship, the perfection of placement, engineering precision, and the pure use of intelligence never fails to mesmerize. *Hail to the Swiss*, I say yes!

Designing and manufacturing Swiss products has given me that sense of Swiss ownership and the desire to continue the tradition, as well. Thank you, universe, for allowing me to design and manufacture under the Swiss brand and culture. Truly appreciated.

Brainstorm Session in Switzerland

High-end Swiss Watch deal "Meeting" going down
at 35,000 feet what a "Meaning"!!!!

Read on for my experience of a "Meeting" at 35,000 feet where I witnessed a high-end Swiss watch deal GOING DOWN by a watch broker sitting right next to me in first-class!!!

Typical flight pattern, New York to LAX, nonstop, pre 911. Routine flight boarding, and that day I got upgraded, thank you!

So, we all started to settle into our seats; I was in 4B, and 4A was open. Then, here comes "Mr. I do not know"; he was a good-looking European gent who was well dressed in a nice Italian suit, very expensive shoes. He was on the phone speaking loudly. With him were two huge bodyguard-looking dudes, both wearing radio "curly coils" behind their ears. I could tell they were either protecting him or escorting him.

One of the bodyguards looked at me, sized me up, and asked that I move for a moment so the gentleman could sit into 4A. The "Mr. I do not know" at the time dude stopped talking on the phone for a moment, also sized me up, and then waved off the bodyguards, saying, "It's ok"; he then sat down next to me, still loud talking on the phone. Then, one of the bodyguards sat 2 seats behind us across the aisle in 6D, and the other bodyguard left the plane. I thought that was   very odd because *how could this bodyguard guy get on a plane that far, then turn around and get off?* Keep in mind, this is pre-911.

I am thinking this guy sitting next to me is either a mob guy, a senator, or an escorted prisoner out on bail!

My senses were telling me that something was going on with this guy, and that he, along with the person sitting a few seats behind me, was special.

I remember sharing a flight once with another exceptional passenger, ex-President Ford. He was surrounded by protective agents, all of whom had the "curl coils". Everyone on the flight was so excited. He had the entire first-class section to himself. He was the last to board the flight and the first to get off. No one was allowed to go to the front of the plane.

Ok, back to my undercover guys. We have taxied at the gate, and this gentleman is still on the phone speaking loudly. I can tell now that he was some type of dealer or salesman on a conference call. He was asking for bids. He was talking numbers, but the numbers were in code – *oh, it was an auction, right on the flight with people listening*. In his mind, since he was speaking in auction code and had a European accent, he probably thought no one knew what he was talking about. But it was clear to me that he was a broker/dealer.

He was going back and forth and back and forth, and you could tell that the number was going higher. Suddenly, he kind of stood up a little, waved, and did a "thumbs up" to the bodyguard in row 6, with a big smile on his face. I couldn't believe this guy had no regard for the people around him, that we could hear everything he was saying. I have been around plenty of Europeans, from Germans, Dutch, UK, Spain, Greeks, French, and Swiss. They are a pretty conservative bunch, except for the Italians... *Italians, I love your flair and lovely exuberant way of speaking. It's so inviting and intoxicating. Love the Italians!*

Meanwhile, the auctioneer was at the peak of the conversation. Whatever was happening, he surely knew only a few minutes remained to complete the deal before they were going to start the pre-flight security videos and tell everyone to turn off their phones.

After much back and forth, he finally said the magic word - "SOLD!" He said the winner's first name and that he would see him in LA with the prize! And then, "sorry, better luck next time" to the others on the call before hanging up.

He stood up again to look back at the bodyguard. He stood as well and came over to us. They high-fived and shook each other's hands "brother style". It was clear that this guy closed the deal, and they were super happy about it. He sat back down and double fisted himself and said, "Yes, baby!!" Like he just closed the biggest deal of the year or won the lottery. Like a guy who just laid a super beautiful woman, whom he had been waiting for months to be with. It was that kind of "Yes baby, I am the man!"

The flight attendants laughed and shook their heads. Clearly, they knew this guy or knew of him. They had allowed the bodyguard to get on and off the plane, and the head flight attendant gave him thumbs up when he got on the plane to deliver his boy.

I couldn't help but wonder *who this guy was and what deal just went down that he closed while sitting next to me?*

The flight attendants started to prepare the flight for takeoff. My now-known-as-a-dealer friend next to me was elated with joy and calming down from his DNT high. He took a few deep breaths to calm his heartbeat, and he wiped the beads of sweat that had built up from his adrenaline. I could see and feel that the "deal monster inside of him" was now quieting, and the real person was resurfacing. Almost like the Incredible Hulk, after an episode.

He turned to me and said, "Well, hello." I said hello, of course, and just let him settle in. I was dying to ask him what was going on with that phone call, and *who the hell are you?* But I just let him be, to calm down. I have been in those types of victory meetings many times with buyers or auctions for computer product deals, so I know how intense it can be to win the prize. You feel on top of the world.

Then the reality of what you just accomplished and the amount of energy you put into it sets in - then you feel exhausted and wiped out.

This is what he was going through. He asked for two glasses of water before the flight took off. The flight attendants brought the water to him with no delay or questions asked. Once again, it was clear that they knew who this guy was before he boarded the flight.

He drank his water, took a few more deep breaths, shook his hands in stress release, and then took a few more breaths. Very clearly, he knew calming techniques to calm himself and to drop his heart rate. I hadn't mastered this technique at that time in my life. Now, I have it down to a science. Breath is the center of everything. Master this, and you can control your surroundings and the outcome of it by the breath alone. It is an excellent practice of Kundalini yoga and meditation.

The flight is now ready to take off, and we are on our way from New York to LA. Awaiting on the other side is my family, and for him the delivery of the "prize". I was still curious about what he was dealing with on the phone that was so important that it had to be done before those doors were closed. My curiosity was now getting the best of me as we reached 35,000 feet cruising altitude. ***The "Meaning" of this "Meeting" has now begun.***

As we reached cruising speed, Mr. Dealer finally settled down, and I was relaxed, as well. Dinner was being served, and all was good. He looked towards me and said Hello again. I said Hello, and we began the usual conversation mode.

He was from Switzerland and introduced himself as a watch dealer. That was very interesting because I worked with the Swiss at the time. The majority of the products we have are our Swiss watches, backpacks, and luggage.

He began with an apology for his loud conversation on the phone and explained that he was on the phone with six guys who are connoisseurs of Swiss watches.

These gentlemen have a competition between them to see who can buy the latest and the greatest Swiss watch directly from the factory before it's made available to the public. He had said watch on his wrist, this prize watch that they had all wanted, and he was going to hand-deliver it to the winner. It was a $350,000 watch ... a Breguet.

To give you an example of the price range for these Breguet watches, this guy had the starter version on his wrist. No wonder he had a couple of bodyguards next to him. You could get your arm chopped off in LA if people knew you had that walking around on you.

BREGUET GRANDE COMPLICATION CLASSIQUE NUMBER 5349 - $755,000

The Grande Complication Classique Number 5349 possesses three patents to protect its superior precision and technological mastery. The watch has more than 570 unique parts in it. It has twin-rotating tourbillons and a platinum case that is lined with baguette-cut diamonds. Even the dial is paved with diamonds.

BREGUET GRANDE COMPLICATION TOURBILLON MANUAL WIND WATCH - $734,000

This watch has a round platinum case and measures 50 millimeters in diameter. It has a transparent case back and a black crocodile leather strap. The face has a silver engine-turned dial paved with 310 diamonds that weighs around 1.62 carats. The numbers are in black Roman numerals. It has blue steel Breguet hands. The bezel, case band, and lugs are paved with 107 baguette-cut diamonds that weigh 30.3 carats. The sapphire crystal is resistant to scratch. The watch is also water-resistant up to a distance of 30 meters.

BREGUET HORA MUNDI - $633,000

The Hora Mundi is probably the first watch in the world to display two time zones simultaneously. It was actually sold to an avid collector of watches. It has a case that is encrusted by diamonds weighing more than 20 carats. The dial also displays the map of the European continent set in sapphires and diamonds.

Back to the story... The dealer further explained that he works directly for the Swiss watch factories. When customers are willing to pay over retail price for the first edition or first run off the production line, he gets involved. He has the end-to-end hook-up. Factory and clients. He gets a 10-20 percent commission off the deal, no questions asked.

I asked him what kind of clients buy these types of watches. He said primarily high-end businesspeople, athletes, lots of Saudis and Europeans who appreciate Swiss-made watches and for whom money is no issue. Their only concern is to have the latest and greatest to add to their collection. It is the same as Sneakerheads or ladies with designer purses.

It is a fetish of style and elegance as well as an investment, as these pieces can easily be resold for cash if needed.

The watch dealer loves his job, selling a high-quality product to high net wealth individuals who genuinely appreciate Swiss art, design, and craftsmanship.

I started to explain to him what I do for Swiss with bags and luggage. He said, "No shit - we are Swiss brothers!" with a smile on his face, and shook my hand. "I have all Swiss luggage and backpacks; I love you guys' stuff. It has the same high quality, Swiss tradition, and great design. You guys are everywhere in the world."

He added, "Listen, anytime you want to make a high-end Swiss watch for your brand, let me know, and I will intro you to the best watchmakers in Switzerland". He gave me his card and said, "I am really glad I met you. It is cool to see someone else on the other side of the pond who cares about the Swiss tradition and the high quality we like to achieve." More small talk followed. Of course, he showed me more of the prize-winning watch he was wearing. It was beautiful. First production run, and he had the first off the line; it would be hand-delivered straight from Switzerland. He said there would be "no "f***ing way" he'd send it by Fed Ex (laughing)!

129

These guys want instant gratification and personal delivery service.

Besides hearing him close the mega watch deal, there was "Meaning" in this "Meeting", now that I knew what the product was, who the clients were, and the price tag for the watch he sold!

The "meaning" reminded me to continue my pursuit to design and think of ideas that people want, desire, and or need. To give them a sense of pride when they use it or wear it. To design products that will help them, even if it's about their fashion sense. The magic is in all of the details. After that meeting, a few designs were created, one of which won the "Good Design" award in 2007/2008 with the help of RKS Design. *Thanks, Ravi S. Dalino Brazilan/Portugal designer for Cosmo 3.0 from Swissdigital*

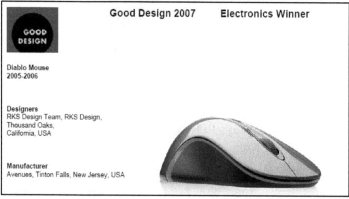

The plane landed in LAX. We exchanged goodbyes, and sure enough, when the door opened up, two more bodyguards were waiting at the door! The bodyguard inside the plane held up the people in first class and asked if I would let his client out first. I said, "sure". Mr. Swiss watch dealer shook my hand and said, "So nice to meet you and good luck designing Swiss." The bodyguards surrounded him, and off he went to deliver the $350,000 watch to the buyer.

CHAPTER 23

YOGA AND MEDITATION

Everyone can benefit from yoga and meditation and can start to use it wherever they are in their life (Christians calm down; God says to love everyone). Adding yoga to your daily life will bring incredible and positive changes in your life. Yoga asanas will, if you practice, help you to burn calories, strengthen the body, mind, and soul, and offer benefits you cannot even imagine. I find it particularly helpful and "healthful" whenever I fly.

Yoga is an ancient system for personal, physical, mental, emotional, and spiritual development. It's good for reducing stress through physical exercises.

Yoga means "union" or "yoke" in Sanskrit, an ancient Indo-European language of India. It means the body, mind, and spirit become as one during quiet, united through the practice of the asanas or postures along with breathing techniques called pranayama and meditation. You can ultimately do yoga by yourself after going to a yoga class for a while or watching yoga videos to visually learn more about it.

You can get in touch with your body's wisdom through the postures, and you will know just how far you want to push or challenge yourself. It's based on a fundamental principle of East Indian Philosophy that there are five layers or dimensions to human existence:

1. The physical frame.
2. The vital body made of prana (life energy).
3. The mind.
4. The Higher intellect.
5. The abode of bliss where inner peace and union with the Divine occur.

Asanas (postures) can release muscle tension, stretch and tone muscles, lubricate joints, massage internal organs, increase circulation, and aid in weight control. Yoga postures are comprised of movement sequences performed while standing, sitting, lying down, or balancing on your head, shoulders, hands, or bending backward or forward and sideways.

In a structural routine, each pose counterbalances the preceding one by stretching and strengthening. You can investigate your attitude toward yourself and your body. It's a very loving thing, which you can learn to do for yourself, and no one else needs to be there. Practitioners report that it has alleviated such conditions as arthritis, scoliosis, back pain, insomnia, chronic fatigue, asthma, heart conditions, and much more.

A typical yoga practice of postures would include warm-up poses before a yoga class or session. Then practice some different standing poses: Triangle pose, hands to feet, standing side stretch pose, stand spread leg forward fold, Warrior pose, tree pose, and Sun Salutation. All these poses can be done in a seated fashion, as well.

You might decide to practice because you heard from friends that their yoga practice reduced their stress and relaxed their bodies. Researchers have found that Yoga actually reduces the level of the stress hormone cortisol. Perhaps your friends shared that their digestive problems have been erased or eliminated or that their conditions of anxiety, depression, or insomnia are no longer present. All these results have been documented in yoga practitioners.

- **Pain Relief.** Many people have found pain relief is a by-product of the type of yoga they have been practicing. They may have found that doing Power yoga, for example, has been effective for them in erasing pain. Bikram Yoga has been beneficial for them because the heat you work under releases toxins from the joints and body.

- **Increased Strength**, mentally and emotionally, is also a by-product of meditating. Being still and breathing slower brings about much clarity, peace of mind, and higher self-esteem. With a yoga practice, it will help maintain weight management because you will burn calories gently.

- **Better Breathing**. Better breathing takes place when you learn to breathe correctly. You take slower, deeper breaths. Relaxation is a natural result, which continues to blossom as you practice. The lungs improve their function, which increases the amount of oxygen (and pranic energy) to the rest of the body.

- **More Flexibility.** You become more flexible. The synovial fluid around the joints is increased for more cushioning of the joints. Muscles along the spinal column are lengthened, over time, with frequent practice. Muscles surrounding the joints and the bones are lengthened and become less tight, so bending is no longer a problem. Stomach muscles are firmer and tighter to act as a girdle for the abdominal cavity (the colon, large and small intestines). The organs and glands are gently stimulated.

- **Improved Circulation** is another reason to practice yoga. The yoga postures (asanas) effectively manage oxygen to flow more proficiently to the body's cells. All glands, organs, tissues, bones, blood, lymph fluids, and spinal fluids are definitely affected and enhanced for the better. By practicing Yoga, you can lower your resting heart rate over time and help issues with blood pressure.

- **Proper Body Alignment** is achieved through the use of postures. Aligning your body helps you manage or eliminate back pain, joint and muscle problems, **and** neck or leg pain.

Yoga will arm you with hope, faith, and practical solutions as a healing tool in your life. Yoga has many benefits, including:

1. Deep Relaxation for the body and mind
2. Stress management
3. Maintaining/developing flexibility
4. Building up of muscle strength and length
5. Strengthening of the respiratory and circulatory systems
6. Improved supply of nutrients to all tissues
7. Prevention and alleviation of chronic illnesses (cardiovascular disease, asthma, depression, arthritis, and others)
8. Correction of faulty posture and its long-term effects
9. Slowdown of the aging process
10. Enhanced power of concentration
11. Promotion of physical and mental well-being
12. Weight loss and maintenance

Having a yoga practice, one that you choose, which feels right for you, helps you focus on the present and live in the now. You tend to release worry about the future and remorse for the past. It allows you to live happily in the present moment, which will create a bright future on its own.

Yoga has been used for thousands of years because of its many and long-lasting health benefits. Maintaining your youth, flexibility, and healing can be done with yoga. The various yoga styles, such as Hatha, Iyengar, Ashtanga, Vinyasa, Kripalu, Bikram, Kundalini, and others are highly beneficial for body, mind, and spirit.

The body systems, including the skeletal system, reproductive system, circulatory system, endocrine glands, lymphatic system, and organs, are healed by the inversion asanas, stretching postures, and backbend and twisting asanas. These can be great for the spine and vertebrae. Of course, check with your doctor first if you have pre-existing back injuries. Taking time to relax in each posture, breathing properly, and not forcing yourself beyond your limit will make your Yoga practice enjoyable.

CHAPTER 24

YOGA IN FLIGHT, THE "MEETING" AT 35,000 FEET AND THE NAMASTE "MEANING"

During my international flights, I have a routine exercise protocol. On a 10-15-hour flight, I always make sure I get up and do yoga to keep the blood flowing. Performing Yoga while flying long distances also keeps my mind sharp and does not allow it to get too foggy.

I will never forget one particular flight because it was so different from the others I had taken from LAX to Hong Kong. There was a center galley in the middle of the plane. It was nice and wide, and the flight attendants put out nice snacks and drinks for the few passengers who got up to stretch their legs. I am always surprised to see how many people never get up to move or stretch their legs or backs on these long flights. It is mind-boggling but also very unhealthy, according to health studies. My suggestion is to move and stretch at least 3-4 times during a 10+ hour flight to get the blood moving and prevent blood clots.

Back to the story.

I was in the galley, and I started my yoga routine, as follows:

Yoga in flight, the "Meeting" at 35,000 feet
and the Namaste "Meaning"

Practicing Yoga on New Year's day 2020 in Long Beach CA

While I was in the middle of doing my routine, a Chinese lady came into the galley with me. She just stood there and looked at me with a smile. This was very unusual to me because in past flights, whenever I have done my Yoga routine, the other passengers passing by or coming into the galley area quickly leave or just watch me do the practice outside of the galley. No one ever says anything.

This Chinese lady watched me, and she said the following. "Hello, very nice. Where did you learn those routines?" I told her it has been a mix over the years in California, Panama, India, China, Taiwan, etc. I have taken many different types of yoga classes with beautiful instructors. My favorite instructor was a lady named Amanda from Equinox in Huntington Beach, California. *Hi Amanda, I miss you.*

Yoga in flight, the "Meeting" at 35,000 feet
and the Namaste "Meaning"

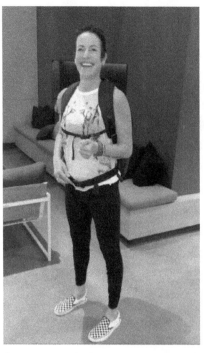

With pure innocence and curiosity, the Chinese lady said, "I have never seen a man do this full routine in an airplane before- especially a black man!" I told her that I cannot sit in those seats, no matter how comfortable, without moving 4-5 times during the flight. She said, "me either" because her back would start to hurt; she also needs to move and do yoga! I was shocked when she asked if she could join me in my Yoga routines. I was so surprised because in all the other international fights I have taken it is almost as if people try to avoid me. Maybe they do not want to interrupt my flow or think I am a weirdo, or it is just plain awkward to talk about what I am doing in the middle or in the plane's back.

I said to her, "Sure!!!"

So, we made space for each other in the galley, and we began the routines. She would call a pose, and then we would do that pose 4-5 times. Then I would call a pose, and we would do that pose 4-5 times. The session lasted a good 30 minutes. We were in sync, just like a yoga class! We were breathing and flowing with ease, right in the middle of the plane!. *You should have seen the faces of the people coming by or the flight attendants strolling by. They were in awe.* One of the flight attendants came by and started to applaud and said, "That is just beautiful. More passengers should do this practice and experience this on a plane. Flight attendants also should do this practice." We both agreed and said thank you as we continued to move in our majestic flow state.

Pose after pose, we moved with healing and grace to soothe our bodies and clear our minds. As we came to our final poses, we said to each other, "Let's just breathe with our hands on our hearts."

We stood there for 5 minutes with our hands in prayer formation over our hearts and our eyes closed, and we just breathed. It relaxed our minds, and we felt our hearts opening up to the 3rd eye, going at 700 MPH and at a higher elevation, to catch the jet stream to Hong Kong.

It was a beautiful practice, session, and a beautiful experience with my new friend from China. Her name was Ming.

I thanked Ming for the partnership in yoga and for speaking to me. It was the first time I felt in sync with my yoga practice in the flight. The experience kind of validated my feeling that the yoga I had learned over the years can be done in any setting, even in the galley of an airplane.

The "Meaning" of this "Meeting" is Namaste.

Namaste. The word **ends** our practice, but whether **we say** it or not, the practice of **yoga is** the embodiment of the word's meaning. ... This reflective moment reminds me that **yoga** transcends language and culture, that connecting mind and body helps us look more deeply into ourselves and at our world.

I will continue this beautiful Yoga practice at 35,000 feet and above. I look forward to the next brave soul joining me in the FLOW State and universal language of the body, heart, spirit, and mind.

Amen!

CHAPTER 25

FOLLOW YOUR DREAMS

Everyone always says, "Follow your dreams!" But not everyone does it. When you are motivated and excited about pursuing your dreams, you'll attract other people who have the same values and interests. The more you surround yourself with high achievers, the further you'll go. Then, when times get tough and it's hard to keep going, hopefully, your friends and family will motivate you to continue achieving.

If you decide to pursue your dreams, you will give hope to others who want to do the same. You can serve as their example and their reason why they should give it a try. You can help them, coach them, and encourage them to keep going as well.

Dreams make your life worth living. They can get you through even the worst days. If you are struggling, your dreams are your reason to keep going. They are why you wake up in the morning and try again.

When you are this motivated, it's tough to fail. If you are very set on your dreams and make sure that you can make an income along the way, you'll be able to provide for your family. Some dreams take longer than others to achieve, but that's what makes the end goal so worth it.

Everyone has their own dreams and their own goals for what they want to achieve in life. Search far and wide for yours and make a promise to yourself that you will start pursuing them. Once you get on the path towards your goal, you will notice a distinct change in how you feel.

All of us have been around people who told us our dreams weren't possible. If and when that happens to you, let that add fuel to your fire. Think about all the people who said it would never happen and go out and prove them wrong. When you accomplish your goal or fulfill your dream, you will be proud of yourself! Your confidence will rise, and you'll enjoy the excitement and the adrenaline that comes with doing something you've always wanted to do.

Life is short. Our days are numbered, so why spend them doing something we don't love? It's time to go for it. Focus on your dreams and make your dreams happen.

CHAPTER 26

THE HISTORY OF
AMERICAN AIRLINES

Amerian Airlines is the world's largest airline by fleet size. With over 950 aircraft bearing the American livery, many passengers in the U.S. and worldwide will be familiar with their aircraft. Let's step back in time and see how American Airlines came to be.

The 1930s

American's story really started to unfold by 1936. After a few years of flying, businessman E.L Cord branded the conglomerate "American Airlines". After putting together a team, American Airlines started working to create a new aircraft. The product was the DC-3 which became American's flagship.

American Airlines DC-3 "Flagship".
Photo: Wikimedia/Cory Watts

The first flights operated between New York and Chicago. The DC-3 allowed American Airlines to transport passengers and their baggage. Previously, American Airlines relied on mail transport to make a profit. The DC-3 changed this, and American Airlines was on its way to becoming a major airline.

As American Airlines expanded their DC-3 service, they also started looking at improving the passenger experience on the ground. The first Admirals Club came about at this time. American also worked to build up New York's LaGuardia Airport, where another Admirals Club was also developed. Back then, the Admirals Club was almost as exclusive as it is today, with invitation-only policies for entry. Later, American did begin offering paid access to their Admirals Club too.

The 1950s

American Airlines had its eyes set on transcontinental operations. For this, they needed an aircraft that could fly from a city like New York to one like Los Angeles in under eight hours. At that time, domestic flights could only be eight hours or under due to crew time restrictions.

American turned to their preferred aircraft manufacturer, Douglas, and the DC-7 was created. The DC-7 was a major success, with American Airlines operating a significant number of this aircraft. The DC-7 was primarily used for nonstop service across the U.S.

American Airlines Douglas DC-7. Photo: Wikimedia/Jon Proctor

In the late 1950s, American Airlines opened the "Stewardess College" in Dallas, now their largest hub. The Stewardess College was for flight attendant training. It was the first official flight attendant training facility in the world.

In 1959, American Airlines began flying the Lockheed Electra. However, soon after starting service with the aircraft, AA flight 320 crashed on approach to New York LaGuardia. 65 out of 73 passengers on board died.

American Airlines Lockheed Electra.
Photo: Wikimedia/Jon Proctor

The 1960s

As new advancements in technology made jet aircraft a reality, American Airlines started flying the Boeing 707.

Jet aircraft were much safer compared to turboprop and propeller aircraft. They also significantly reduced flying time and were a favorite for major airlines.

Also, in the 1960s, American Airlines introduced the first electronic booking system for passenger reservations.

American Airlines made history in 1964 when they hired Dave Harris, the first African-American pilot to work for a commercial airline.

American Airlines Boeing 707. Photo: Wikimedia/Perry Hoppe

The 1970s

At the start of the decade, American Airlines merged with Trans Caribbean Airways. They thus started offering flights from the U.S. to the Caribbean.

Continuing American's trend of 'innovative hiring', Bonnie Tiburzi became the first female pilot for a major American Airline when she started flying for American.

In 1978, the Airline Deregulation Act was formed. The airline industry was now deregulated in areas such as route creation, new airline establishment, and fares. This, essentially, turned the American aviation market into a free market.

Trans Caribbean Airways and American Airlines merged in 1970.
Photo: Wikimedia/Christian Volpati

The 1980s

In 1981, American Airlines instituted the first airline loyalty program. The name AAdvantage has stuck with the program since its inception.

Following airline deregulation, American Airlines opened a hub at Dallas/Fort Worth International Airport. This was closely followed by new hubs in Chicago, San Jose, Raleigh-Durham, and Nashville. During this time, American Airlines focused on building a hub-and-spoke model and began transatlantic services out of Dallas.

American Airlines flew a wide variety of aircraft in the 1980s, including various 747 models and the 767-200.

American Airlines 747-100. Photo: Wikimedia/Ted Quackenbush

The 1990s

American Airlines continued to grow in the 1990s. And, on March 27, 1991, American Airlines crossed the one billionth customer mark.

American Airlines gained a hub in Miami after taking over Eastern Air Lines' Latin American routes. At the same time, they discontinued their hubs at San Jose, Raleigh-Durham, and Nashville.

In 1997, American Airlines banned smoking from all of their flights.

Then, in 1999, American Airlines partnered with British Airways, Cathay Pacific, Canadian Airlines, and Qantas to found the Oneworld alliance.

American Airlines 777-200ER in Oneworld Livery.
Photo: Wikimedia/Alan Wilson

The 2000s

American Airlines flights 11 and 77 were involved in the September 11th attacks that forever changed aviation. In the years following the event, American Airlines continuously lost money until finally earning a $58 million profit in 2005.

During this time, American Airlines inaugurated many services worldwide to destinations such as China and India.

US Airways merged with America West in 2005.
Photo: Wikimedia/Paul Carter

Then, in 2005, US Airways merged with America West Airlines. Doug Parker, CEO of America West, was retained as part of US Airways management after the merger.

In 2008, the economic downturn hit American Airlines hard. Due to lower profits, AA shut down their Kansas City maintenance station and downsized operations at their Puerto Rico hub.

During this time, American Airlines also began to refresh their fleet with new Boeing 737s and Airbus A320 family aircraft. This came after disputes with the FAA regarding maintenance on their aging MD-80 fleet.

American Airlines purchased 737 aircraft to replace their aging MD-80s. Photo: American Airlines

The 2010s

American Airlines officially inaugurated its transatlantic joint venture with British Airways and Iberia Airlines in 2010. In addition, American Airlines strengthened their joint venture with Japan Airlines and inaugurated multiple services to Tokyo-Haneda.

Expanding from Dallas, American Airlines began flights to Seoul, Shanghai, and Hong Kong. This further solidified American's hub status at Dallas, where they remain the dominant carrier.

In 2011, however, AMR Corporation, the parent company of American Airlines, suffered some financial troubles. They filed for bankruptcy, and American Airlines began a cost-cutting campaign to return to profitability.

In 2013, it was announced that American Airlines and US Airways would merge, creating the world's largest airline by fleet size. As a result, the American Airlines brand would be retained. American also revealed a new livery and logo. After some negotiations with the Department of Justice and the Department of Transportation, US Airways and American Airlines were officially granted a single operating certificate in 2015. The new CEO of the merged airline was former America West CEO Doug Parker.

American Airlines merged with U.S. Airways in 2013.
Photo: American Airlines

U.S. Airways flew its last flight, number 1939, on October 16, 2015. 1939 was symbolic, as that was the year that US Airways was founded.

The Future

American Airlines remains the largest operating airline in the world. AA is one of the 'big three' American carriers, maintaining dominance in several key markets, including Dallas, Charlotte, Philadelphia, and Miami.

As of now, American Airlines is in a solid position to keep flying. With brand new 787 and 777 aircraft, American Airlines is looking to expand its long-haul operations and phase out older aircraft with newer, more efficient aircraft.

American Airlines 787. Photo: American Airlines

CHAPTER 27

AMERICAN AIRLINES 3,000,000 MILES CLUB ... AND COUNTING

I will never forget the day when I reached the level of the American Airlines 3,000,000 Miles Club ...and counting (today it is 3,321,915 miles). I felt *what an accomplishment in my life to see the world and have an opportunity to mix business with pleasure on American Airlines.* Thank you, AA, you have been wonderful to me, and I thank you for your excellent service.

It is wonderful to see different cultures, diverse people, and beautiful art, museums, parks, seas, and mountains, while you are flying. Especially if you fly over Alaska, the Grand Canyon, or large mountain terrain. It is just spectacular. I have no idea why people keep saying there is a global crowding issue and Mother Nature is in trouble. When you fly for 5 hours and see nothing of buildings or people, it is just unbelievable. I am genuinely amazed at how much of the world is not inhabited by people.

I remember flying over Alaska, and the pilot told everyone to look at the sunset reflecting off the glaciers. It was the most exciting and most beautiful sight I have ever seen. People cried about the sheer magnificence and beauty when they saw the sunset from the plane's windows. It was just mesmerizing.

In this, I embrace our beautiful world and all its elements: the air, the sun, the water, and the sand. These are all the things man needs in life to survive. In the past, this is how we lived – today, some Indigenous tribes still do. They lived off the land and appreciated Mother Nature. It is interesting how things are going back to "Farm to Table" and authentic organic living. I like the trend, just as long as people are honest and not just placing a marketing label on the item saying that it is organic, and it is not!

Life is constantly evolving, and Mother Nature has adapted to what we have done to her. She knows how to change, and she will continue to survive as she should. Man needs to get his act together and fast because Mother Nature shows us how powerful she can be every year.

Through hurricanes, fires, earthquakes, volcanoes, and such, she shows her power. And if you happen to have the misfortune to be in her path at the time, you will feel that power. There is nothing man can do to stop or control Mother Nature. We can only embrace or run from it.

Man is in trouble, not Mother Nature.

I have learned from veteran-flyer colleagues that there are some useful strategies to stay fit, healthy, and "sane" while flying so many miles:

Fly 1 or 2 days earlier than your appointment, depending on if it is international or domestic. It also depends on the client and preparation that is needed before the meeting.

- Try to stay 1 day after your appointment, to rest or see the city in the country that you may have never visited before. *Since you are flying such a distance, it is ideal to take in the area and the people.* It is always good to know coffee shops, restaurants, transportation methods, important local places, and most importantly, the culture of the people, museums, local sites of interest, and or future vacation spots.

- Sleep as well as you can. In other words, stay in a nice upscale hotel.
- Don't drink heavy alcoholic drinks. Instead, drink wine, light beers, and lots of water.
- Essential oils are a must, but make sure the bottle's size meets the TSA standards for carry-on. Find the one that works best for you. Try **lavender** to relieve stress, **peppermint** to boost energy and aid digestion, and **sandalwood** to calm nerves and help focus. **Rose** is used to improve mood and reduce anxiety, **chamomile** to improve mood and relaxation, **tea tree** to fight infections, boost immunity, and lemon aids digestion, mood, and headaches.
- Apply Neosporin around your lips and nose. **Neosporin** contains antibiotics that kill bacteria on your skin and is used as a first aid antibiotic to prevent infections from minor cuts, scrapes, or burns.
- Also, bring hand sanitizer, vitamins, prescription medications, melatonin, and antibiotics with you.

Particularly when traveling, I do not recommend over-the-counter cold medicine. Instead, if you feel a cold coming on, have a Hottie Tottie (bourbon or whiskey mixed with honey, lemon juice, and hot water) or use a Neti Pot (a container designed to rinse debris or mucus from your nasal cavity). Flush that sh**t out of your nose; medicines just coat it. Don't be afraid to blow your nose, as often as needed. *As a* *matter of fact, the only (over-the-counter) thing I see that works is Mucinex. This is a fantastic congestion clearer, and it doesn't make you feel fuzzy.*

Exercise. I only try to book hotels with a gym and/or swimming pool. Swimming to me is my travel therapy. Once I land and get settled in, I head to the swimming pool and dive right in. As soon as I hit the water and start to swim and breathe, all signs of jet lag vanish. It is something in my body's movement, the breathing, and the free flow that energizes me right away and places me back into balance. No energy drink, supplement and or oral remedy can do this for me. Even running on a treadmill and pumping some weights does the trick. *It's good to keep the bod in shape, at my age!*

Because I travel overseas so often for business, I have created a particular routine for endurance during my long international flights:

Pack as lightly as possible. *I have my packing down to a science. I have learned what clothes to bring and what not to bring. A jacket, hat, and scarf are 'must-haves' in cold weather.*

Arrive 3 hours before the flight. (Especially out of LAX). After boarding the plane, I do the following:

- Call my parents, text message my daughter, and close family friends. Why, why not? Tomorrow is never promised. *Smokey New Mexico, remember?*
- Get settled into my seat.
- Check my surroundings.
- Update my 'To Do' list for things to accomplish on that trip or in the future (both work and personal).

Now, it's time to get physical. For example, if it is a 15-hour flight, my journey goes something like this:

- 1st 2 hours, have a meal and catch up on things on computer or phone.
- Yoga moves
- 2nd, for 2-4 hours, sleep
- Yoga moves
- 3rd, for 5 hours, I watch 2 movies
- Yoga moves
- 4th, for 2 hours, I have another meal and finish up any work or update notes.
- Yoga moves
- 5th, for 1 hour, I sleep and/or read or talk to someone, if they are open to it.
- 6th, for 1 hour, I prepare to land.
- Total 15 hours.

All in all, my life of travel has been amazing. I have interacted and established beautiful relationships, cultivated a sense of travel pride, and experienced the world outside of Westside DA Carson. The La Raza is my heart, but the world is a blank canvas onto which you get to paint a new vision of life. You alone can create a masterpiece that is unique to you and meant to be cherished for the rest of your life.

Everyone should travel somewhere out of their comfort zone; it is a priceless experience. Embrace it, breathe it and honor it in pictures, your memories, and in your heart.

Once again, thank you, AA, for the 3,000,000 Miles Club. See you at the 4,000,000 mark. *I would like to have a free worldwide trip, please!!!!*

Much love to all in the travels. Respectfully, Les.

CHAPTER 28

MS RASTA GIRL

Scan QR code with phone
To See Chapter Preview

I leave you with one last great story. I love Jamaica and all that it stands for: the music, the mixed cultures, the warm greetings, the beautiful, exotic yet simple dances, the food, the open hearts, and beautiful voices. *Come on over here mon, for a moment, and let me tell yah something, I won't bite yah.*

When I met Ms. Rasta Girl on the plane at a wonderful "Meeting" at 35,000 feet, the "Meaning" was instant friendship, instant openness to diverse cultures, and just a great understanding of the human race. Amazingly, you can meet a person in this cramped space and time, with nowhere to go but the bathroom or galley, and nothing to do but mingle - or in this case, talk for 2 hours straight!

I went to do my routine yoga relaxation moves and to the bathroom, and there she was, walking from the back of the plane to the middle bathrooms by the galley. I named her "Ms.

Rasta Girl". She had beautiful long dreads from the top of her head to the middle of her calves, and her face had a natural glow as she swayed down the aisle - almost as if she were listening to some Rasta music. She was dressed in a traditional Jamaican wool top of beautiful burgundy, browns, greens, and orange with baggy jeans and wool socks. Both arms were adorned with beaded bracelets and multiple rings on each finger. She also wore several necklaces made from beads and crystals.

You could tell right away Ms. Rasta Girl was a true spirit-walker on this earth. When she reached the bathroom area, she stayed in line and waited patiently. She saw me and gave me a nod of acknowledgment as she watched me finish my last yoga routine pose. Once again, while other people either looked at me in wonder or just passed by quickly, Rasta Girl nodded at me.

It's so interesting to feel someone's energy. You know that they want to talk to you and want to talk to them; there is this hesitance inside you, and you can feel it inside the other person as well. As Rasta Girl neared the restroom, it was that same nod and a brief smile. I smiled back. She went inside to utilize the facilities, and when she came out, I could see a slight delay in her steps as she moved towards the back of the plane. It was almost as if she were saying, *Ok, yogi guy, this is your time to talk to me. I'm gonna give you a few minutes to make the first move to talk to me before I head to the back of the plane and take my seat.*

Her beautiful glow and friendly smile made it clear that she had a warm and inviting soul, so I took the opportunity and said, "Hello, how are you?"

She said, "Fine, I was just tired of sitting on the plane. When I saw you out of the corner of my eyes doing your yoga routine, I thought it was so beautiful and fascinating that you were doing it right in the middle of the plane! So, I decided I should get up and stretch my legs too, to try to relieve the pain from all this sitting."

I told her, "Yes, I agree with you; there's no way in the world that I can sit on this flight for 15 hours and not get up and move, or go to the bathroom, or try to stretch. I would be a total nut case by the time I got to the other side of this flight."

She laughed and said, "That was amazing to see you doing yoga in the middle of the plane, and I wondered to myself, where did you learn that? I really do not see that many Black men doing yoga, especially on a plane! You know it would be an ego thing for our brothers. So I can see that either you do not have an ego problem, or you're very carefree in your practice, which is absolutely beautiful."

I thanked her and said that I also want to represent our brothers as we travel globally to show our vast culture is expandable into all beliefs and experiences.

She told me, "I also practiced yoga and kundalini. It is one of my favorite activities to do, and I've been doing it for many years." She also said that she was a professional musician and music teacher. Plus, she taught piano, guitar, and African dance. I was absolutely fascinated learning this about her.

This opening allowed the "Meeting" to begin the journey between us toward discovering and understanding different cultures and lifestyles in the world.

Ms. Rasta Girl was a fascinating young lady, as I came to find out. She had traveled the world from the time she was 14 years old, making it her life's journey to experience different cultures in India, Africa, Jamaica, and many other places in the world. It was beautiful to see an Earth-walker who wanted to discover the diverse cultures of the world.

As a born non-conformist, she decided early in life to defy convention and see all the places in the world that raced into her mind and that she could afford to visit.

We began to tell our different travel stories throughout our lives. The stories lasted for 2 hours! She told me about her long stint in India, where she went because she wanted to help the children. She saw the poverty there, and even though she knew it was their karma, she felt compelled to help. She really needed to lower her ego to help these children in need, connect with them, and show them how to make music. So, she taught piano and different types of dances in India that she had learned along the way.

She saw what I saw in India, where there's a beautiful sense of pride in their lives, no matter the economic status. I saw from Mumbai to Bombay to Bollywood, Delhi to Calcutta, some of the poorest people I have ever seen. She had seen the same. I saw people living in shacks. I saw people living in pure poverty who were still able to smile. I saw children outside, playing and running around and tagging each other, without any shoes; some didn't have any clothes, and yet they were still running around enjoying themselves. There were no Nintendo games, X-Boxes, or computers. It was just children playing with sticks, wooden things, and dirt, and it was just absolutely amazing that they still had beautiful smiles on their faces and laughter in their hearts.

Rasta Girl said to me, "I saw the same; it's a blessing that, even in those types of conditions, people can still be happy, believe in "God" (keep an open mind for a moment Christians -smile) and believe in a purpose for their life. They know they may not be the richest people in the world, but it costs nothing to be rich in the heart and in the spirit. They are content with the beauty of family, and being able to get together, pray, dance, and sing together is worth much more than any money could ever provide."

I was taught a valuable lesson on this topic. I told her, "When I was in India, I told a driver that what I saw in Calcutta was horrible and sad." Seeing this, I was in tears my first time traveling there and asked the driver, "Why doesn't anyone help these people?" He told me, "Les, you have to remember, everyone has their karma path, and we should not judge them by your path or others' path experience. They could be much happier than you or even a super-rich person, in their heart, not from their material possessions. Remember, Americans see by their standards, but even in America you have people who live on this level, and they could be happier in their own karma path." I left it alone because, in a way, he was right. I was thinking from my ego, status, and view of life.

Next, I asked Ms. Rasta Girl where she learned African dance. She told me that she had traveled all over Africa;

Nigeria, Kenya, Botswana, and Johannesburg. In these different places, she absorbed their song dance styles and immersed herself in each and every culture. She relished the gifts of each country. I really was so touched and fascinated by her choices to broaden her experiences. It was absolutely beautiful.

Ms. Rasta Girl had gained the opportunity to go to Africa from her uncle. She jumped at the chance because school was so uncomfortable for her as a young girl. She found Africa fascinating and so different from LA and San Diego, where she originally came from. Ms. Rasta Girl was a light-skinned, long-haired black girl, who was very beautiful and very open to what she was seeing, and she tapped into it very quickly.

She asked me if I knew any African dances, which I didn't, even though I've seen how African people dance on trips to Ethiopia, Morocco, and Johannesburg. It was fascinating how these mixed cultures moved their bodies, so different from the "get down" boogie ways of LA and New York!

Their movements were like a beautiful breath of fresh air flowing to the beat. It was almost as if God's gift was given to them, especially to the women - incredible to see in the moment. I will never forget the way one woman, named Khadli, in Morocco, danced.

She asked me if I wanted to see one of the African dances that she had learned. I said, "Girl, we are in the middle of a plane." She goes, "What? You're doing yoga in the middle of the plane, so why can't you do an African dance?" She was right, and I just started laughing. But sure enough, there she went. Oh, my goodness gracious, right in the middle of the plane with everybody there, this girl went into full-on African dance mode. It was terrific, and she started doing something like this little beatbox, African drum playing while she was dancing. Then, she started singing an African song, with the passengers in the plane watching. This experience took my plane experiences to a new level. I have never met such a free spirit who didn't care if other people were watching. I would love to express myself like that and experience what she had learned in her journeys. *That would be so cool.*

When she finished her beautiful African dance, she just started smiling and laughing with pure joy. I said, "That was amazing, Rasta Girl." And she goes, "Thank you so much."

I said, "Wow, I cannot believe that you learned that beautiful African chant and dance!"

She said, "Yes, I know many dances - I've learned from different cultures what they mean and how to display them correctly, putting the right chant with the right dance. Being a musician who plays guitar and piano, I have an ear for music. So, it's very easy for me to pick up the different rhythms and aspects of the music and how they relate to the body."

I said, "You know that you are a very rare woman."

She said, "Yes, I feel very different, and I find it very strange that I have an instant affinity for these types of activities. It's almost as if my soul craves them. Other people think that I'm very, very odd and awkward. But I'm in my own little world when I hear the music and the beat! As soon as I hear these songs, I'm drawn into them, almost as if I become a part of them."

I said, "I could see that. I could see it in your eyes, and I can see it in your movement. I could see how free and carefree you became. You were not doing a routine; you were actually letting the rhythm take control of you."

She said, "I'm going to sing you a little African song. You may not understand the words, but it's about nature, it's about the sunrises and about the sunsets. It's about the plains of the wild." And, she started singing this beautiful African song that was mesmerizing. It was angelic, and it almost brought me to tears, right there in the middle of the plane. It just showed me, once again, how stuck we are in these earthly ways. But these easy little melodies bring you back to the simple nature of how things were and how things should have been before we built this concrete world that we have today.

While I thanked Ms. Rasta Girl for her performances over the past two hours,the lady that was sitting next to us said, "Guys, I know you are having a great time, and it has been very entertaining to us, but it is time to get some more sleep." The lady was right. We got so carried away with our stories and dances and singing that we forgot about the other passengers near us! *Oh, my how time passes when you are having fun.*

Ms. Rasta girl and I exchanged our information and said we would keep in touch to trade travel stories in the future.

We hugged, kissed cheek to cheek, and went to our respective seats for the rest of the flight. I was so thankful to have experienced such a free spirit, even more free-spirited than me!

It was a great "Meeting" with Ms. Rasta Girl, and the "Meaning" is very clear. "Follow your dreams, enjoy the world, and don't be afraid to show your spiritual colors. Dance, sing, be silly and live to the beat of the music.

See you in the future, I am sure, Ms. Rasta Girl. Love and peace to you.

IN CONCLUSION

R emember, life is too short, tomorrow is never promised, so live life to the fullest today. Tell the people in your life that are close to you that you love them before walking out the doors. If you have a sense of spirituality in your life, thank God that you woke up to see the day, no matter your religion or belief.

When flying, after reading this book, you will probably remember a unique time that touched your heart and soul and how it changed your life or someone else's life. ALL IS WELL and as it should be because we are not entirely in control. You create the experience by opening up to it and embracing it fully if you are awake.

Love and Peace to you and happy journeys in your beautiful skies. *Be free like a "bird"*...

Email me if you would like to share a unique story, trustinfaith@gmail.com

Les Dotson

ABOUT THE AUTHOR

L es Dotson was born in Inglewood, California, in 1965. He currently lives in Long Beach, California and is also a Panama Resident.

Les' beautiful daughter, Alicia Leslie Dotson Crespin, is married to Ryan Crespin. The couple has one child, Les' beautiful granddaughter, Kayla Crespin.

Les' parents are Earl and Nancy Dotson; he has a twin sister, Lisa Chandra Dotson and a younger brother, LaMar Cedric Dotson.

Les is a Designer/Innovator/Businessman/Brother of Life/Child of God. He is fully aware of his life purpose, giving back and providing humanitarian solutions that help the whole world.

CPSIA information can be obtained
at www.ICGtesting.com
Printed in the USA
FSHW020421160621
82401FS